LOVE YOUR
DOG!

Everything you need to know to raise a healthy, happy pet

SHEILA BUFF

Copyright © 1994 by The Triangle Group, Ltd.

Published by
World Publications, Inc.
455 Somerset Avenue
North Dighton, MA 02764

Produced by The Triangle Group, Ltd.
227 Park Avenue
Hoboken, NJ 07030

Editorial: Jake Elwell
Design: Tony Meisel
Printing: Cronion S.A., Barcelona

ISBN 1-57215-004-7

Printed in Spain

Contents

CHAPTER ONE

Choosing Your Dog

The first step in caring for a dog is choosing one. Ideally, you could carefully consider this vital step, thinking at length about why you want a dog and what type it should be. You would then select it after a long and thorough search. This approach, of course, is only rarely feasible. Many happy dog owners obtained their pets by adopting a stray that wandered into the yard, choosing a puppy from a neighbor's litter, or by taking in a dog whose owner could no longer care for it. Even in these cases, however, some basic questions need to be asked before you make a commitment to a dog.

First and foremost, why do you want a dog? If you want companionship and uncritical love, and if you are willing to provide the company and return the love, that is reason enough.

Do you want a watchdog? In general dogs are protective of their homes and owners, but a dog that is primarily a pet should not be expected to provide a major deterrence. If security is your primary concern, a family dog is not the answer. Professionally trained guard dogs are used successfully in security work, but these dogs are not pets.

Do your children want a dog? Parents sometimes get a dog for their children hoping it will teach them responsibility. A dog is indeed an excellent companion for older children but generally children under the age of six see a dog as just another stuffed toy and cannot be expected to contribute significantly to the dog's upkeep. Plan to care for all the dog's needs yourself. Even if your children are old enough to take care of the dog, remember that it is you who must handle vet trips, vacation arrangements, and other details. A family with an allergic or asthmatic child should probably forego a dog.

Do you have the time—or are you willing to make the time—to care for a dog? The care of a typical medium-sized dog takes about two hours a day. That sounds like a lot of time, and it is: three daily walks of at least twenty minutes each (or one longer walk and two short ones), twenty minutes or so for feeding, treats, and filling the water bowl, another forty minutes for grooming, playing, petting, training, and generally enjoying your dog. Even routine visits to the veterinarian take time and a dog that becomes sick or injured will need extra vet visits and additional care. And you will have to go on giving all this time to your dog for its entire lifetime, easily twelve or more years. If you, alone or in combination with your family members, can't make a genuine time commitment, think very carefully before getting a dog.

A dog is also a financial commitment, though one that is generally within the means of anyone. While the purchase price of a pedigreed dog can run well into the thousands, the cost of a good puppy from a reputable breeder is usually far less. The price for adopting a dog at an animal shelter is minimal and the cost of a mixed-breed puppy from a neighborhood litter is usually free. Annual costs for dog food, supplies and miscellaneous expenses for a typical dog will run several hundred dollars—less for small dogs, more for big ones. Veterinarian bills can add up, but excellent free or low-cost medical care for your dog may be available through animal shelters and humane organizations.

Once you're sure about your ability to give a dog the time and attention it needs, a number of other issues need to be thought through.

Purebred or mutt? The words purebred and pedigreed refer to dogs that are alike in appearance—and often in temperament and behavior—as a result of selective breeding. In other words, over the course of centuries humans have selected individual dogs with desirable physical and behavioral characteristics and allowed them to breed only with dogs that have similar characteristics. Eventually, this process has produced such distinctive breeds as the Great Dane and the dachshund. A purebred dog is one that has only dogs of that particular breed in its ancestry. The written record of a purebred dog's ancestry is called its pedigree.

The American Kennel Club today recognizes over 130 different dog breeds, divided into several categories. Some breeds are more common than others. The Labrador retriever, for example, is a well-known and very popular breed, while the pharaoh hound is rather rare.

The major advantage of a purebred dog is that its size, appearance, and behavior can be predicted with a fair degree of accuracy. This knowledge helps you select a dog that will fit well into your household and lifestyle. If you live in a small apartment and don't like to go for long walks, a small dog that is content to chase a ball around the living room is obviously more appropriate than a large and rambunctious dog happy only when chasing rabbits.

Dog breeds and their characteristics are described and illustrated in many books. If you want a purebred dog, peruse these books but do not stop there. Look at actual dogs of the breeds that interest you. If you see a dog of the breed being walked, talk to the owner—dog owners love to talk about their pets. Visit local dog shows and breeders. You can also see purebred dogs in the movies and on television. Be careful here. Don't let your enthusiasm—or the enthusiasm of your children—for a stage dog lead you into purchasing an inappropriate pet. Dalmatians, for example, are large, energetic, difficult to train and are not necessarily the best choice for a family dog.

Pedigreed dogs also tend to have more physical and behavioral problems, sometimes as a side effect of their make-up and sometimes as a result of over-breeding. Because shih tzus and other small dogs with flat faces have protruding eyes, they are more prone to eye injuries and infections; golden retrievers are prone to cataracts. More importantly, uncaring breeders sometimes allow dogs with physical or temperamental shortcomings to breed and pass on the undesirable characteristics. Such purebred dogs not only do not conform to the breed model in appearance and behavior but also may inherit physical deformities that can lead to serious health problems.

Of course, selecting a good dog to begin with and caring for it properly will prevent most problems with pedigreed dogs before they start. (For more on selecting a puppy, see chapter two.)

A dog whose father is one breed and mother another is called a cross-breed. These dogs usually inherit distinct features of each breed; thus the appearance of the adult dog can be predicted to a certain degree. Mixed-breed dogs, more familiarly known as mutts, are dogs whose ancestry includes a variety of unknown breeds. Cross-breed and mixed-breed dogs offer many advantages over purebreds. Often a cross-bred dog combines the best features of both parent breeds without the physical drawbacks. In general, mutts have far fewer health and behavior problems than pedigreed dogs. The size and future appearance of a mixed-breed puppy is hard to predict when the father is unknown. Mutts tend to be sturdy and intelligent with even temperaments; they are not likely to be "high-strung" or have irremediable behavior problems.

Long or short hair? Both long- and short-haired dogs shed. Long-haired dogs tend to shed in the spring and fall, while short-haired dogs tend to shed year round. Obviously, long hair is more visible than short hair. And a large dog has more hair to shed than a small dog. A few dogs, such as poodles, don't shed, but must have their fur clipped every six weeks or so. Some dogs, such as borzois, have long coats that must be carefully brushed every day to keep them in good condition. (See chapter five for

A long-haired fellow like this requires special care to maintain his coat. Make sure you're up to the task.

more information about grooming your dog.) In general, long-haired dogs deal with cold weather better; conversely, short-haired dogs are more comfortable in hot weather.

Male or female? Unless your dog is a valuable pedigreed animal that you plan to breed, it should be neutered before its first birthday (see chapter four). Neutering basically resolves many of the behavioral issues that lead people to select a male or female dog. A female dog is usually a little faster to walk than a male, since she will empty her bladder quickly. All other things being equal, male dogs in general are more aggressive than female dogs. Ultimately the choice of a dog should really depend on the individual animal's appeal to you, not its sex.

Puppy or older dog? Puppies are adorable, but as they grow up they require a fair amount of effort from their owners. A puppy must be carefully watched, trained, housebroken, and taken to the vet. The work and occasional destruction involved in raising a pup are offset by the special bond that develops between you and your dog.

If you don't have the time or energy to deal with an active puppy, consider adopting an older dog. Animal shelters are full of wonderful, well-behaved adult dogs seeking loving homes. Older dogs are generally housebroken and healthy with established behavior patterns. Their destructive puppy days are behind them. These dogs will bond with you very quickly and adapt well to your household.

TRAINING YOUR DOG

This book mentions specific aspects of training only where that is relevant to dog care. Numerous excellent books on the subject of dog training are readily available at your library and local bookstore. A much better approach to dog training is to participate in an obedience class, usually offered by an animal-welfare organization such as the American Society for the Prevention of Cruelty to Animals (ASPCA) or a local animal shelter. The cost is almost always little or nothing—just a few hours of your time over a few weeks—but the benefits are enormous.

CHAPTER TWO
Puppy Care

The squirming, roly-poly little ball of fur you choose as your new puppy requires some special attention. The time and money spent now are excellent investments in the future health and happiness of your pet.

CHOOSING THE PUPPY

Your first decision, as explained in chapter one, is what kind of dog to get. If you opt for a purebred animal, the next step is to locate a puppy of the breed you want. It is almost always best to purchase a puppy from a reputable home-based breeder. Puppies born and raised in a home environment are usually healthy and well-adapted to living with humans. To find a breeder in your area, check with the American Kennel Club. The staff can help you locate breeders and breed clubs near you. Your local veterinarians may be able to refer you to a nearby breeder. Also check the classified columns of local newspapers community bulletin boards. Often a breeder advertises the availability of a litter of puppies using these inexpensive methods.

As a rule, it is best to avoid pet shops when buying a puppy. The animals sold in these stores sometimes come from large breeding operations where quantity is often more important than quality. A puppy in a pet store is cooped up in cage and receives little human attention and love at just the time when it needs lots of both. It may also not receive proper health care. Finally puppies raised this way often never really adapt to living in a household.

Once you have a few breeders' names, start by calling for a visit. Not all the breeders on your list will necessarily have puppies available. Even if all the pups in a litter are already spoken for, or if there are currently none, the breeder should be willing to let you come by to meet any puppies and the bitch (mother dog) and the sire (father dog) if he belongs to the breeder. Most breeders will welcome your visit—beware of those who are evasive about a visit to the premises.

A good breeder provides clean, pleasant surroundings for the dogs. The environment should be friendly and relaxed. As you visit with the breeder, you will be asked about yourself, your family, and your lifestyle. Responsible breeders sell their dogs only to customers they think will provide good homes. The parent dogs should be calm, friendly, and healthy. The appearance and temperament of these dogs will give you a very good idea of what their puppies will be like.

Deciding which pup to select is the next big step. There are two areas to investigate: health and temperament.

A healthy puppy *looks* healthy. Its eyes are clear and bright, its ears are pink and clean, its nose is soft and moist. Any discharge from the eyes, ears, or nose signals a potential health problem. A bad smell or black debris in the ear can indicate ear mites, which are not really a serious problem, but can be signs of trouble. The puppy's soft hair should be smooth and glossy, with no scabby or hairless areas.

It's almost impossible to have dogs and not to have some fleas, but a lot of fleas on a puppy may indicate that a kennel has low cleanliness standards. Bowel movements should be firm, with no suggestion of diarrhea; check the puppy's rump for staining, discharge, or bad odor. Feel the puppy's abdomen near the bellybutton. A lump in the area indicates an umbilical hernia, a condition that may need to be corrected by surgery later.

Look in the puppy's mouth. The gums should be pink and healthy-looking. The puppy should breathe easily and quietly. Avoid a puppy that is panting a lot or coughing.

Next, observe the puppy as it plays and moves. A healthy puppy is active and sometimes clumsy. Excessive activity may be a sign of hyperactivity while a very clumsy puppy may have hip dysplasia or some other problem.

Assess a puppy's temperament by how outgoing and friendly it is. A good puppy will respond positively to you by sniffing, licking, and inviting you to play. It will not mind being handled and petted, although it will probably squirm away quickly. Avoid a puppy that seems excessively shy, frightened, or shrinks away from your hand.

Puppy shoppers are often drawn to a small fellow that seems sad or quiet. Hard as it is to resist the soulful eyes of a withdrawn puppy, steel yourself. The reason the puppy is so quiet could well be that he is sick or defective in some way. That appealing smallness probably means the pup is the runt of the litter. It's cute, but it may have serious problems later on.

Purebred puppies are often advertised as "AKC registered." This does not mean that the American Kennel Club is in any way involved in the transaction—registration is not a puppy seal of approval. AKC registration only means that the breeder has completed a form recording the puppy's breed, sex, color, date of

Life on a puppy farm.

birth, the breeder's name and address, and the registered names and registration numbers of the puppy's dam and sire. That the puppy's parents are both registered purebreeds guarantees that the puppy is also a purebreed. If the puppy's parents are both outstanding examples of the breed, it's likely that the puppy will be the same. In some cases, however, the puppy, though perfectly healthy, is considered an imperfect example, usually for aesthetic reasons—the puppy may not be exactly the right color, for instance. In such cases, the breeder will sell the pup with a limited AKC registration, at a lower price, if you agree that you will not breed the dog and perpetuate its "undesirable" qualities.

Most breeders raise their dogs for love, not money, but you are participating in a business transaction when you buy a puppy. In exchange for your money and promise to give the pup a good home, a breeder provides an AKC registration and a bill of sale that guarantees the puppy is healthy, has been wormed, and has had shots at the correct ages (see below for more on vaccinations). Take your new dog to the vet within two days of bringing it home. Reputable breeders will refund your money and take back the puppy if any serious health problems are discovered.

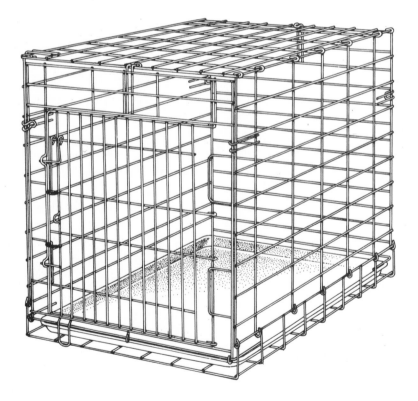

You may find it necessary to purchase a cage for your dog. Shop around for one that is sturdy and well suited to the dog's size and strength.

Remember that price is not everything. Puppies from championship stock will generally be more expensive than puppies from less exalted parents but these dogs will not necessarily make "better" pets. Select your pet based on what you can afford. Breeders usually ask a fair price and can't afford much negotiation. Don't take an inferior or unhealthy puppy even if a bargain price is offered. Sometimes, however, you will be offered a lower price on a pup for a good reason—because it is the last one left or has some minor defect in its appearance, for example.

Of course most puppies are mixed-breed treasures that cost almost nothing to adopt. To find a mixed-breed puppy, check with friends and neighbors, look on community bulletin boards, in the "Free to Good Home" classified ads in your local paper, and at local animal shelters. When selecting a mixed-breed puppy, the same considerations of health and temperament detailed above should apply. One drawback to a mixed-breed puppy is that it is difficult to predict its adult size and appearance, even when both parents are known. This is amply compensated for by the vigorous good health of most mixed-breed dogs.

PUPPY CARE

Your new puppy should be taken from the litter between the ages of eight and twelve weeks. A puppy at this age will bond deeply with the new humans in its life and adapt well to its new home.

Introducing the puppy. Your new puppy has just been removed from the security of its mother, littermates, and familiar surroundings. It has been placed in the arms of huge strangers (you) and taken on a car ride only to end up by itself in a strange, new place. He's feeling bewildered—but he's also curious about his new home and eager to meet his new family.

The new puppy needs a warm, safe environment, and gentle handling. Warmth is important—puppies don't have their adult coats yet and can easily get chilled. Provide a warm spot for the puppy in a draft-free area away from doors leading out of the house. Place a washable old blanket or a few large towels in a cardboard box with high sides to make an excellent and inexpensive puppy bed. Puppy "crates" (wire cages or dog transporters) are a more permanent alternative.

Puppies have seemingly boundless energy and love to play; they are also growing rapidly and need lots of rest. A puppy will frequently be playing zestfully one minute then fall sound asleep the next. Particularly when the puppy first arrives, there is a temptation to play with it constantly and shower it with attention. Try not to let this go on for long. The sooner the puppy becomes part of the normal household routine, the better.

Handle the puppy carefully. Support the rear legs with one hand and the chest and front legs with the other. Young children tend to be rough on puppies, not realizing that they are delicate and need gentle handling. A puppy can be seriously injured if it is squeezed too hard, dropped or dragged around by a child.

If you already have a dog, introduce the puppy in a quiet way. The adult dog will sniff the puppy and may growl at it. This is normal; the adult dog is telling the puppy who's boss. Over the next few days, there may be more growling and even some snapping as the older dog asserts its dominance, but the two will probably also play or even sleep together. The two dogs will eventually develop a close relationship, but patience may be needed in the meantime. Sometimes the older dog will become depressed or lose its appetite when a puppy arrives and grabs all the attention. Make sure your adult dog knows you still love him!

Puppyproofing. Puppies, like toddlers, are insatiably curious. Just as a household with a baby must be childproofed, a household with a puppy must be puppyproofed. Puppies will get into cabinets, medicine chests, and storage areas so secure them with childproof latches (available at hardware and housewares stores). Cover unused electrical outlets with childproof plugs. Puppies can electrocute themselves by chewing on electrical wires; raise or remove lamp cords, extension cords, and the like wherever possible. Remove toxic house plants such as mistletoe, dieffenbachia, and ivy.

Any veterinarian will be happy to regale you with stories about the amazing objects he or she has removed from the stomachs of puppies. Keep small objects—paper clips, rubber bands, game pieces, buttons, and the like—away from the puppy, just as you would keep them from a small child. Provide the puppy with sturdy dog toys of rawhide, leather, or plastic. An old baseball glove makes an excellent toy as does an old athletic sock with a ball tied into the toe. Avoid stuffed animals and anything that can have parts chewed off and swallowed.

Most importantly, be aware of the puppy's whereabouts. So small and active, your puppy can get underfoot easily. If you step on or trip over him, at best you will be subjected to heartrending yelps; at worst, you could injure the dog or yourself. Puppies are escape artists with a fascination for forbidden rooms and the great outdoors. Always make sure all gates and doors are firmly closed. Young puppies are perfectly content to stay in their boxes, playing with a toy or sleeping for long stretches. Put the puppy in his box whenever he is likely to get underfoot.

Feeding. A sudden change in a puppy's diet can upset its digestion. Ask the original owner what the puppy has been fed,

Like young humans, puppies adore toys. A chew-toy such as this adds valuable exercise for growing muscles.

and make any changes gradually.

Your puppy is growing rapidly and needs to eat at frequent intervals and requires a diet higher in protein than an adult dog's. Any of the commercial dog foods formulated specifically for puppies will provide the correct balance. Many owners find that dry food (kibble) mixed with a little bit of canned food is a tasty and economical approach.

It is extremely important to remember that your puppy is not a human. A high-protein, high-fat diet is unhealthy for a person, but it is exactly what a puppy needs to grow up properly.

Very young puppies should be fed four times a day at regular intervals. Place the food in a shallow dish on a sheet of newspaper or washable mat (puppies are very messy eaters). The puppy will eat its fill and then walk away. If the pup eats all the food in just a few minutes, increase the amount you offer. Remove any leftover food after about 15 or 20 minutes. As the puppy grows, feed more food but offer it less often.

An alternative to frequent feeding is self-feeding—leaving a bowl of dry food where the puppy can always reach it. The pup feeds himself when he gets hungry. Self-feeding is simple and effective, but only if the puppy is the only animal in the house. If you leave food out constantly, other dogs (and even cats) in the household may eat it and the puppy could go hungry.

Always make sure that the puppy has fresh, clean water in a shallow bowl at all times. Puppies enjoy milk, yogurt, and other dairy products. Their digestive systems, however, are not really meant to handle dairy products after they are weaned. If your puppy gets diarrhea from milk or other dairy products, stop offering them.

Eating stimulates the digestive system of a puppy. Take advantage of this to housebreak the puppy naturally. After it eats, immediately bring the pup outside (or place it on newspapers). Praise the dog lavishly when it relieves itself.

Worms. Virtually all puppies get intestinal parasites—worms—as a normal if unpleasant part of growing up. (See chapter 6 for more information about parasites.) Symptoms of worm infestation in puppies include vomiting, diarrhea, lethargy, and loss of appetite. The symptoms may come and go, with the pup appearing fine one day, sick the next, and fine again the day after. Promptly take the puppy to the vet as soon as symptoms appear. Bring a stool sample so that the vet can determine if worms are the problem and, if so, what type they are. The treatment depends on the type of parasite, but it usually consists of medication that is injected or given as a pill. Your puppy will feel better almost immediately. Do not use commercial worming preparations unless the vet specifically tells you to.

Vaccinations. Puppies should have their first vaccinations between the ages of five and eight weeks. At this time shots for preventing distemper, parvovirus, and parainfluenza shots are given. At 14 weeks the distemper, parvovirus, and parainfluenza are given again along with the first vaccinations against hepatitis, leptospirosis, and rabies. (See chapter four for more information about these illnesses.) At 15 months, the entire six-shot sequence is repeated again. The vaccines are combined so that the dog receives only one or two shots.

A double-bowl dish like this is ideal—it keeps food and water in a single place.

CHAPTER THREE
Feeding Your Dog

Good nutrition is essential to your dog's good health and long life. By following a few simple guidelines your dog will be well-fed and happy.

SELECTING THE RIGHT FOOD

Commercial dog foods fall into three categories: dry (kibble), semimoist, and canned (wet). When fed in the recommended amounts, any one of these foods provides a complete and tasty diet for your dog. Most owners end up feeding their dog some combination of the three types. Kibble has the great advantage of simplicity. Simply place the kibble in the bowl and offer it to the dog—no fuss, no preparation, no refrigeration. Kibble is ideal for dogs that self-feed because the food can safely be left out all day. Kibble is also the least expensive way to feed your dog. Although a dog will thrive nicely on a diet of plain kibble, many owners flavor the kibble by topping it with a bit of canned food or a few table scraps.

Semimoist food generally consists of pellets or chunks of processed material packed into a pouch. For the owner, portion control is easy: just open the pouch and empty it into the bowl. Storage is easy as well, since no refrigeration is needed; a bowl of semimoist food can be left out for the dog with no fear of rotting. Semimoist food tends to cost a bit more than kibble or canned food.

Canned dog food is available in a wide variety of flavors and sizes. The choice of flavors is more for the owners than the dogs; your dog will happily eat the same food day after day for its entire life and never once complain of boredom. The range of sizes has a more practical purpose. Buy the size that you are most likely to use up within a week of opening. Cover cans of wet food and store in the refrigerator.

Most veterinarians recommend a diet of plain kibble supplemented by small amounts of moist or canned dog food. This approach is economical and provides a nutritionally complete diet. It also keeps the size of bowel movements to a minimum, an important consideration, particularly for large dogs.

There are numerous dog food brands available, ranging from

generic store brands to premium brands sold only by veterinarians and pet-supply stores. To select the brand that is best for your dog, check the labels on the containers. Look for a feeding statement that lists the nutritional adequacy of the product—by law, this information must be provided. Most vets agree that the best way to determine the nutritional adequacy of a food is by test feeding, not laboratory analysis.

If you change brands or change the mixture of food you offer your dog, do so gradually to avoid digestive upsets. In general, a dog that eats a lot of kibble will drink more than a dog that eats mostly semimoist or canned food. *MAKE SURE YOUR DOG HAS PLENTY OF FRESH WATER AT ALL TIMES!*

A word of caution. Your dog is a carnivorous mammal with a digestive system designed primarily to process meat. Although it is possible to design a healthy vegetarian diet for a dog, it is not recommended. By the same token, a low-fat diet, while desirable for humans, is not necessarily good for your dog. If you are concerned about these controversial issues, discuss them with your veterinarian.

HOW MUCH FOOD?
Perhaps the greatest health problem among American dogs is obesity. Dogs tend to be fed too much and exercised too little. For a long and healthy life, feed the right amount of dog food and avoid offering people food.

Feeding directions are listed on the packaging of the dog food brand you choose. Experience will probably show that the recommended amounts are a bit too high for the average dog.

As a general rule, an adult dog needs to eat 30 to 40 calories per poundweight per day. More active dogs may need more food, while inactive or older dogs may need less. When feeding kibble, a general guideline is one cup for every ten pounds of body weight; for moist food 1.5 ounces per pound of body weight. For canned food, the general guideline is one 16-ounce can for every ten pounds of body weight. Of course, if you feed a mixture of different food types, or if you offer a lot of table scraps, the amounts must be adjusted accordingly.

Experiment to find the food amounts for your dog. If your dog is consistently leaving food over, reduce the amount you offer. If your dog seems consistently hungry and is not overweight, offer more food. You will soon find the amount that leaves your pet satisfied.

Young puppies need to eat four times a day. As the puppy gets older, feedings can be reduced. By the time the dog is about six months old, a morning and evening feeding should suffice.

Many adult dogs continue on this pattern, but others do best with just one meal a day, either in the morning, or more commonly, in the early evening (about 5 or 6 o'clock). Try to keep to a regular schedule to avoid dietary upsets.

SPECIAL CASES

The guidelines above are for healthy adult dogs. As discussed in chapter two, a puppy has different nutritional requirements that must be met. By the same token, very active or working dogs need more food than the typical household pet and inactive dogs need less. A discussion with your vet and experience will help you determine the right diet for these dogs.

Pregnancy. A pregnant dog has special dietary needs. She is eating not just for two but more likely for five or six! A dog's pregnancy lasts about 63 days. Her need for extra food starts almost at once. Start by increasing her food by about 20 percent during the first few weeks of the pregnancy, adding more food if she still seems hungry. The most important time for a good diet and plenty of it is in the last trimester of the pregnancy, from about the 35th day onward. By this point a pregnant dog should be eating about 50 to 60 percent more than usual. Your dog needs lots of extra protein now. Give her more of her regular diet supplemented with semisoft cheese (cheddar, for instance), cooked eggs, meat, chicken, and liver. Your vet may also recommend a vitamin supplement. As the pups grow within her womb, they press on the mother's abdomen and stomach. At this point it is best to offer the dog small, frequent meals.

Lactation. After pups are born, the mother's nutritional needs soar as she produces the milk they need to grow. During the next few weeks, it will be impossible to overfeed your dog. She will eat three times more than usual—and then some. In addition to making sure she has plenty to eat, make absolutely certain she has lots of fresh water. You vet will probably recommend a vitamin supplement during lactation.

Older dogs. As your dog gets older, his metabolism slows down and his digestion becomes less efficient. In general, older dogs need less food. Consult your vet to determine what your older dog's caloric intake should be. It may be time to consider switching to a dog food formulated for older dogs.

With an aging digestive system, your older dog may begin to suffer from flatulence. To a degree, the unpleasant aroma is inevitable, but you can reduce the problem by feeding the dog several small meals a day rather than one big one.

Obesity. It's as hard to put your dog on a diet as it is to put yourself on one. With dogs as with people, weight loss is accom-

Make sure your dog always has water available.

plished by eating less and exercising more. Most vets recommend a diet that is lower in nutrients but high in bulk so that the dog doesn't feel hungry all the time. Commercial dog foods designed for this purpose are the easiest way to go, but they are only half the battle. You must resist giving the dog milk and other dairy products, extra treats and table scraps, and see to it that he exercises more. Try substituting marrow bones, rawhide treats or raw vegetables for cookies and biscuits.

Diabetes and other problems. Dogs with diabetes and some other health problems needs special diets. Your vet will explain the requirements to you and help you determine how best to meet them. The right diet in these cases goes a long way toward keeping the dog as healthy as possible.

BONES AND TREATS

Should you give your dog bones or not? It depends. Dogs need and enjoy the chewing exercise a bone provides, but they can get the same results by chewing rawhide or nylon bones. On the other hand, uncooked beef marrow bones and knuckles are usually perfectly safe for dogs. Any bone that can splinter, however, should definitely be avoided. Chicken bones, rib bones, and bones from chops and steaks should never be given to the dog.

An amazing number of dog treats and biscuits are available. Crunchy dog biscuits are a good snack for your pet. They are nutritious and enjoyable and help keep the dog's teeth clean. Don't overdo, however. Five or six biscuits a day is plenty. Many

The canine pantry—"wet" food, dry food and treats.

dogs like rawhide treats of various types—these are much lower in calories than dog biscuits but are more expensive.

Avoid giving chocolate, ice cream, and sugary treats in general—dogs are not able to easily digest these foods. However, dogs do enjoy fruits and vegetables. Try offering an apple, some cold baked potato, a carrot, or a broccoli stem.

Rawhide bones—available in a wide spectrum of shapes and sizes—are a favorite of many dogs.

CHAPTER FOUR
The Veterinarian

The professional help of a veterinarian is needed to keep your dog healthy. Your dog needs vaccinations, preventive medication, and a regular checkup to stay in the best possible health.

CHOOSING A VETERINARIAN

It's probably best to choose a vet who is located near your home. Check your local telephone directory to find the names and addresses of nearby practitioners. To select among the available vets, decide first if you prefer a solo or group practice. A one-person office means you will always see the same doctor, but he or she may not always be available. In an emergency, you may be referred to another doctor. In a group practice, several veterinarians work together. They may be available more hours a day, and a member of the practice is usually on call for emergencies. On the other hand, the waiting room may be crowded and you may not see the same doctor every time. There are pros and cons to both types of practice, and the choice is a matter of personal preference.

If you must choose among several different veterinary practices, ask friends and neighbors with dogs about the local vets. A referral based on experience may help you decide. In addition, visit the offices and see for yourself.

In an emergency, you may be unable to reach your vet. Long before the need arises, make a note of the address and phone number of the nearest emergency clinic.

Good veterinary care need not be expensive. If you can't afford a vet, check with your local animal shelter or humane society. These organizations can generally help you get free or low-cost medical care for your pet. The vet's bill for a serious problem can be large. Your vet should discuss the financial aspects of your dog's care with you honestly. Most vets will make payment arrangements that are manageable for you.

ROUTINE VISITS

Once your dog is past the puppy stage (see chapter two), a routine annual visit to the vet is all that most dogs need. At these visits, your dog will get a yearly booster shot called DHLPP. This vaccination prevents canine distemper, hepatitis, leptospirosis, parainfluenza, bordatella, parvovirus, and coronavirus. A rabies booster is needed every one to three years, depending on the health regulations in your area. In addition, the vet may recommend vaccination for kennel cough (tracheobronchitis), Lyme disease, and tetanus.

Another important part of your dog's yearly vet visit is a stool check for intestinal parasites such as hookworms. Always bring a fresh stool sample with you to the vet.

The vet will take a blood sample to check for heartworm, a dangerous parasite that is spread by mosquitoes. If your dog doesn't already have heartworms, he or she will prescribe a preventive medicine (prophylactic).

The vet will also check the dog's overall physical health, looking at the eyes, ears, mouth, rectum, and genitals. He or she will check the dog's coat and skin and feel for lumps and other possible abnormalities.

SPECIAL VISITS AND EMERGENCIES

If your dog becomes ill or is injured, a special visit to the vet may be needed. As a general rule, your vet will arrange to see the dog that day. If the problem seems to be intestinal, be sure to bring a stool sample. In an emergency, bring the dog to the vet or to the nearest emergency clinic immediately (see chapter seven for more on emergency care). If possible, call ahead to let them know you are coming and what the problem is.

Make a note of the dog's symptoms, being as precise as possible. If the dog has been taking any medication, bring the container along. The more information you can provide the vet, the sooner a diagnosis and treatment plan can be found.

Sometimes a dog with a very serious or unusual problem requires the care of a specialist. Your regular vet will refer you to the right practitioner.

Hospitalization. Whether your veterinarian's practice is large or small, most can accommodate an overnight stay by a sick dog. If your dog needs hospitalization for longer than that, you can be sure he will get good care if the hospital is fully accredited—ask to see the appropriate accreditation documents. If your dog needs routine medication or is due for a heartworm pill while he is in the hospital, be sure to give the drugs to the vet.

NEUTERING YOUR DOG

One heartbreaking visit to an animal shelter will convince you that there are far too many unwanted dogs in the world. Do your part to help—neuter your pet. You and your dog will both be happier for it.

Spaying. A bitch (female dog) is neutered by the surgical removal of the ovaries and uterus, a process called spaying. The procedure is usually quite simple, and complications are rare. Indeed, many bitches go home the same day or after an overnight stay, and are fully recovered within a week or less.

Most vets agree that a bitch should be spayed before she goes into her first heat (sexually receptive period) but not before the age of six months. The best time for spaying is between six and nine months of age, although the operation can be performed at any age as long as the dog is not in heat. It is not true that a bitch should be spayed only after her first heat or after she has had puppies! Besides sterilizing the dog, spaying usually improves her health. Spayed bitches rarely get breast tumors, and of course do not get infections and other problems of the reproductive organs. In addition, spayed bitches do not develop false pregnancies.

Castration. Male dogs are neutered by the surgical removal of the testicles, a process called castration; it also sometimes called fixing or desexing. As with spaying, the procedure is simple and safe, and recovery is brief. Castration is generally done between the ages of six and nine months, although it can be performed at any age. Do not project your own feelings about castration onto the animal. An unfixed dog will always be in the grip of his hormones, attempting to roam in search of females. Sadly, most lost dogs are males who have wandered off on the trail of a bitch in heat; these dogs are also the ones most likely to be hit by cars. A castrated dog is much easier to control. He will generally be quieter and less aggressive, although he is still a perfectly good watchdog and companion.

Many animal shelters and humane organizations offer free or low-cost neutering. For your sake, for your dog's sake, and for the sake of all animals, neuter your pet.

A healthy puppy needs regular visits to the vet.

CHAPTER FIVE

Dog Care Basics

Your dog has daily needs—exercise, feeding, and love—that require your attention. Your dog also needs regular grooming and occasional special care. For the most part, you can easily provide all your dog's needs, from the routine to the unusual, with very little difficulty.

EXERCISE

The exercise needs of dogs vary considerably with the individual. As a rule, younger dogs need more exercise than older dogs. Beyond that, generalization is very difficult. Many small dogs are surprisingly sturdy, for example, and will cheerfully accompany you on a three-mile walk. Other small dogs are perfectly happy to get their exercise chasing a ball around the backyard or in the living room. The important point is that dogs receive regular exercise so they do not become overweight. Even worse, unexercised dogs are unhappy. Restless and bored, they are likely to develop behavior problems.

Most dogs do well with a good morning walk of about 30 minutes, an early evening walk of about 20 minutes (after the dog is fed), and a shorter late-evening walk. This program meshes well with an ordinary work schedule—the regular exercise of walking a mile or two a day is good for you and for your dog.

Collar and leash. Your dog should wear a neck collar at all times. A collar fits properly if you can easily slip two fingers between it and the dog's neck. In addition, you should have a chain collar (sometimes mistakenly called a choke collar) made of metal or tough fabric. Most vets and dog trainers agree that chain collars are an effective and humane way to control your dog on the leash. Attach the leash to the dangling loop of the chain collar. Chain collars can be used on any sized dog, although some owners of small or very sedate dogs prefer harnesses.

Strap leashes (sometimes called leads) come in varying lengths. Most trainers recommend a woven fabric leash of about 48 inches—avoid chain leashes. An alternative to the fabric leash is a retractable leash of variable length, extending to about ten feet long.

Always walk your dog on a leash. Among other advantages, this keeps your dog from wandering into traffic, getting lost or stolen, eating rubbish, and being a nuisance. As a rule, cities and suburban areas have leash laws.

When walking your dog, keep up a comfortable pace, but allow the dog plenty of time to sniff around. A dog's sense of smell is hundreds of times better than a human's. Dogs rely on their noses in much the same way we rely on our eyes.

Especially in the morning your dog, will probably have a bowel movement when the two of you are out for a walk. Local laws and common courtesy require that you clean up after your dog. This is easily done with a piece of old newspaper or a plastic bag. Remember, dogs can spread illnesses and intestinal parasites through their feces. By cleaning up after your dog you are helping to keep your neighborhood healthy.

Weather. If the weather is extreme in some way—very hot, cold, wet, or windy—keep your walks short. Your dog will be happy to cooperate. In fact, if it is raining heavily your dog may not want to go out at all. Some dog owners put coats or sweaters on their dogs in cold weather. Although the dogs look very cute, in the majority of cases they do not need the coats. Unless the dog is old, frail, sick, or very small, a coat will probably make it be overheated and uncomfortable.

Road salt can pose a real problem for dog owners, because the salt gets into the tiny cracks in a dog's paw pads and is quite painful. Even big, tough dogs are sometimes reduced to sitting on the pavement waving a paw pitifully in the air. To relieve the pain, move the dog off the salted area and onto grass or snow. If possible, rub the paw with a handful of snow to get the salt out. As a preventative, try placing a very thin layer of petroleum jelly on the dog's pads just before going out. Booties to protect the paws can be purchased in pet-supply houses. Your dog won't like them, but the alternative is worse.

Kennels and dog runs. If you leave your dog out for long periods in a fenced yard or dog run, always be sure the dog has free access to fresh water. Provide shelter from the sun, rain, and cold. A snug dog house is ideal. Be sure it is the right size for the dog: not too large and with an adequate opening. Place an old blanket or some towels inside.

Dog trainers don't usually recommend leaving the dog out on a chain or rope. The dog can easily tangle itself in the chain and hurt itself. Invisible fencing is an expensive but effective alternative to dog runs and chains. A buried wire around the perimeter of your property gives your dog a mild electrical shock through a special collar if he crosses the "invisible" fence. The dog quickly

With leash properly fastened, the dog is ready for a long walk.

learns to stay within the boundaries.

Identification. Your dog should have an identification tag listing his name and your name, address, and phone number firmly attached to his collar at all times. A license tag (required by most municipalities) and a rabies vaccination tag should also be attached to the collar. Check your dog's ID tags every now and then, since they sometimes fall off and disappear. In addition to an ID tag, some dog owners have a number painlessly tattooed on the dogs inner thigh or abdomen. The idea is to give the dog an indelible form of identification that helps prevent theft and loss. If you are interested in tattooing your dog, consult your veterinarian.

GROOMING

Some dogs require elaborate grooming while others hardly need any. Most short-haired dogs such as Labrador retrievers require little more than the occasional bath and nail clipping. Curly-coated dogs such as poodles need to be clipped every six to eight weeks. Dogs with long coats (Afghan hounds and Old English

Leashes and leads come in many colors and styles. Dog's name and phone number is an ideal security precaution.

Modern version of the classic dog collar. Note hi-tech plastic clasp and embroidered name for security.

sheepdogs, for instance) need to be brushed frequently.

Grooming your dog starts with making sure his skin and coat are in good condition. A good diet is the first step. If the dog's skin or coat seems dry, dull, or flaky, it may be that he is not getting enough fat in his diet. Try changing to a different brand of dog food. You might also try adding a teaspoon of wheat germ oil to the dog's food each day, or adding a cooked egg. A poor coat can also indicate an underlying illness. Consult your vet.

Regular grooming, particularly when the dog is shedding, is important for good coat health. Most dogs shed some hair more or less year round. Many will shed their heavier winter coat when the weather warms in the spring; the hair may come off in tufts or clumps. Heavy shedding can be irritating to dogs, leading them to scratch and perhaps damage their skin. A good bath and thorough grooming at this time of year will make your dog much more comfortable.

Grooming. A variety of tools are needed for grooming your dog. A double-sided grooming brush metal bristles on one side and nylon bristles on the other is good for all around grooming. A metal carder brush is useful for breeds with a thick undercoat. Very long-haired dogs are brushed with a rake. A steel comb, grooming mitt, or hound glove can be used for short-haired dogs. Sharp, curved steel scissors are useful for trimming hair. A wide range of grooming supplies can be found at pet-supply stores.

Brush your dog vigorously, getting all the way down to the skin. Be sure to brush around the back legs and anal area and to brush out the tail. Don't be alarmed at the amount of hair that comes off. Use the scissors—carefully—to trim long-haired dogs around the anus and around the eyes. If your dog has drooping, hairy ears brush out the ear flaps and trim the hair short. Try to tease apart clumps of matted hair with a steel comb. If this doesn't work, use the curved scissors to cut the mat away. Your dog will be much more cooperative about brushing if you start when he is a puppy and do it on a regular basis. Many dogs enjoy the attention and pleasant sensations of being brushed.

Professional grooming. It is sometimes easier to hand grooming over to a professional. If you own a poodle or another breed that needs regular clipping, or if he is too large or uncooperative to groom yourself, professional grooming is a good alternative. Vets offer grooming services or a can refer you to qualified groomers in the area. Also check your telephone directory and ask your fellow dog owners.

The groomer's premises should be clean, well-equipped, and odor-free with spacious cages and runs for dogs awaiting grooming. The staff should be friendly and professional. Many owners drop their dogs off for grooming in the morning and pick them up later in the day; some groomers offer pick-up and drop-off service. Since the dog will be indoors all this time, be sure to take him for a good walk in the morning. Tell the groomer exactly what you want done and mention any relevant medical and behavioral problems. If the groomer is an employee, offer a tip when paying.

Baths. Unlike humans, dogs rarely need to bathe. Regular brushing is enough to keep a dog's skin and coat clean and in good condition. When a dog is shedding heavily, has gotten very dirty or smelly, or has a bad flea infestation, however, a bath may be in order. Even so, try to avoid baths. If your dog has gotten very muddy, for instance, simply let the mud dry and then brush him thoroughly—the dirt will come off easily. Don't bathe your dog more often than once a month; too-frequent bathing can lead to a dry skin and coat. And don't bathe puppies younger than four months old.

To give your dog a bath, you need a good supply of warm water, a sink or tub equipped with a spray head on a flexible hose, a very mild shampoo (baby shampoo or a special dog shampoo), and several large towels. Because no dog actually likes getting a bath, you may also need more than one person, all wearing old clothes.

Select a warm, sunny day for the bath if possible. Place the dog in the tub and wet him all over with warm water; be sure to soak through thick fur and dense undercoats. Use a small amount of shampoo to lather the dog all over with your fingers, starting at the rear. Be especially careful around the head. Avoid getting shampoo into the ears and eyes. Rinse thoroughly to remove every trace of soap. When you are done, the dog will probably shake himself vigorously. Follow this up by rubbing him down briskly with towels, removing as much moisture as possible. Keep the dog in a warm, dry, draft-free place until he is completely dry. Brush him out well after he is dry.

Skunks. If you live in a rural or suburban area, your dog may have a losing encounter with a skunk. Even if you have never smelled skunk before, you will have no doubt as to what the problem is. The faster you deal with the situation, the better. A traditional and very effective method is to bathe the dog in tomato juice, and lots of it—you will need at least a gallon. Follow up with a regular bath. Vets and pet-supply stores carry special skunk shampoos that are effective but expensive. No matter what you use, your dog will continue to give off a faint whiff of skunk on damp days for weeks afterward. To avoid the same fate yourself, wash the dog wearing disposable gloves and old clothes you

An assortment of reel-type leashes which adjust to changes in your walking needs.

The brush—a must for your dog-supply box.

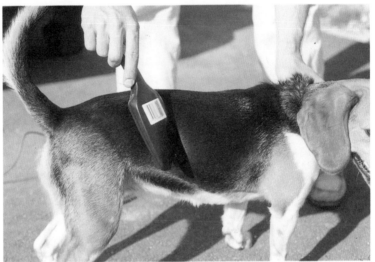

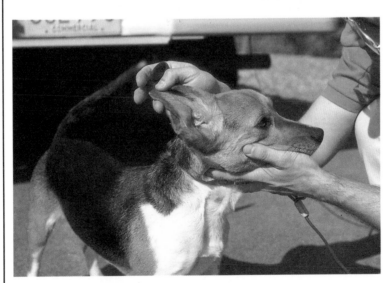

Take your time, be gentle but thorough, and brushing your dog will be a pleasure for both of you.

don't mind throwing out.

Nails. Your dog has four toes on each paw; each toe has a nail. In addition, your dog probably has a vestigial toe called a dewclaw about halfway up the back of each front leg; the dewclaws also have nails. Most dogs naturally wear down their paw nails just by walking about. The dewclaws, however, never touch the ground and can grow very long and pointy. In addition, inactive dogs don't wear their paw nails down naturally.

When necessary, use a special dog nail-clipper to cut the dog's nails. Be sure the clippers are sharp and clean. Quickly cut off just the very tip of the nail, being careful not to cut into the quick. When in doubt, cut too little, not too much. Infections of the nail are painful and very hard to clear up.

Teeth. Dogs clean their teeth naturally by chewing on bones and hard dog biscuits. Even so, their teeth can build up tartar, which leads in turn to bad breath. Clean your dog's teeth occasionally (about once a month or so) by wiping them gently with a damp gauze pad dipped in baking soda or salt. In serious cases of tartar, your vet can clean the dog's teeth under anesthesia.

FLEAS AND TICKS

No matter how good a housekeeper you are, no matter how meticulously you groom your dog—no matter what you do, your dog will have fleas. The most you can hope to do is control the situation.

Fleas are more common in warm weather, but your dog may scratch even in the winter. Because fleas are so tiny, they are hard to see. The most obvious sign of fleas is the sight of your dog scratching and biting himself. Look also for flea dirt—small black specks of flea droppings in the coat and on the skin. Check the dog's back, particularly near the neck and base of the tail, and on the abdomen.

You must take two steps to rid your home of fleas. First, the fleas on the dog must be removed. Second, the flea eggs and larvae that will become a future generation of fleas must be removed from the area.

A number of options are available to rid your dog of fleas. A flea dip or bath is quite effective, especially for serious infestations. The dog is bathed using a special shampoo containing a flea-killing chemical such as malathion or pyrethrin. Flea dips are usually effective for several weeks. The chemicals are powerful, however, and must be handled properly. Read the labels carefully and follow the directions.

Flea powders can be dusted onto the dog; the treatment must be repeated twice a week or so. Flea sprays are also effective;

again, the treatment must be repeated at intervals. Always avoid getting the powder or spray near the dog's face.

Flea collars are an effective approach. Several different kinds using various chemicals are available. Don't fit the collar too tightly. Observe the skin around your dog's neck carefully for the first week or so after putting on a flea collar; if an irritation of any sort develops, remove the collar and consult your vet.

Herbal flea collars and brewer's yeast are traditional, non chemical approaches to flea control. There is little scientific evidence that they are effective.

Your vet may suggest anti-flea medication such as Proban or Pro-Spot. These prescription medications are safe and very effective. Follow the instructions carefully and give the medication only at the proper intervals. Do not use any other flea-control products at the same time. When in doubt, call the vet.

The next step in your flea-control program is to eradicate flea eggs and larvae. A single female flea can lay up to 200 eggs. Start by treating all the animals in the household, especially cats, for fleas, even if they are not scratching. Next, wash all pet bedding thoroughly in hot water and detergent. Vacuum the entire house thoroughly. Immediately remove the vacuum bag and throw it away. Flea bombs are very useful for killing fleas, eggs, and larvae. Read and follow the instructions on the container! If you are reluctant—as well you might be—to use a powerful insecticide bomb in your home, ask your veterinarian about Siphotrol, a special household spray for killing flea eggs.

Flea complications. Many dogs are allergic to fleas making their bites even itchier. The dog scratches or bites at the area especially hard and cuts the skin. Bacteria can then get into the open skin and cause an infection called a hot spot. Typically, a hot spot is a raw, round, weeping sore on a patch of skin with the hair missing. Hot spots usually appear suddenly and are more common on dogs with thick coats.

Hot spots need prompt treatment to break the allergic cycle and to prevent further infection. Watch for hot spots particularly during the peak flea season of late summer and particularly if your dog has had hot spots in the past. If you see a minor hot spot, cut away the hair and clean the area immediately with an antiseptic. If the hot spot is large (bigger than a quarter), or seems infected, a visit to the vet is needed. A visit to the vet may also be needed to break the allergic cycle, usually with an injection of a steroid medication.

Aside from the maddening itch they produce, fleas also carry dog tapeworm. To avoid flea problems, always practice good flea control!

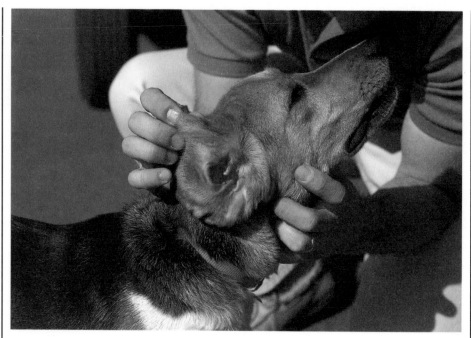

Check closely for fleas and ticks, especially arount the collar and in the ears.

Canine dentistry being performed by a professional.

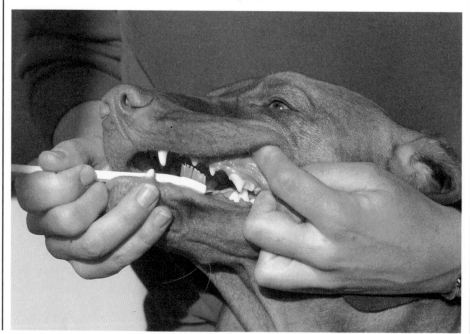

Dogs' teeth should be checked regularly.

Frequent exercise keeps you both healthy.

Ticks. Ticks are small, eight-legged pests that bore into a dog's skin and suck its blood. When the tick is full, it drops off. The bite area then becomes itchy and inflamed. Ticks can give your dog illnesses such as Lyme disease and tularemia and should be removed as soon as you spot them.

Although a tick can attach itself anywhere on a dog, the most common places are around the lips, ears, feet, and tail. The peak tick season in temperate areas is usually the late spring and early summer, but dogs can pick up ticks at any time. Ticks are most commonly found in brushy or grassy areas.

Check your dog often for ticks. If you see one, keep looking—there are probably more. Ticks must be removed by pulling them off; don't wait for the tick to fall off by itself. To remove a tick, first put on disposable or rubber gloves if possible. Soak a large cotton ball in rubbing alcohol and press it against the tick for a few minutes. This makes the tick relax its grip on the skin. Next, use the cotton ball or tweezers to grasp the tick very firmly, as close as possible to the skin. Pull the tick out steadily in a straight line, making sure to get out the head and barbed mouth parts. Apply an antiseptic to the area. Discard the tick and cotton ball and wash any implements. Wash your hands well if you didn't wear gloves.

TRAVELING WITH YOUR DOG

Most dogs enjoy traveling in the car, although some are markedly more enthusiastic than others. Follow some common-sense rules to make car travel safe for you and your dog.

The dog should ride in the rear passenger compartment of the car. Train the dog to sit or lie on the seat or on the deck of a station wagon. Do not let your dog ride with his head or nose sticking out the window—serious injury may occur. And never put the dog in the trunk!

If you must leave your dog in a parked car, even for a few minutes, *leave the windows open.* Even on a cool spring day, the interior of a car parked in the sun with the windows closed will become unbearably hot very quickly. Many dogs have suffered unnecessarily or even died from heatstroke after being closed up in a car on a hot day.

Carsickness is common among puppies and young dogs; it usually lessens as the dog gets older. Your vet can prescribe medication to prevent carsickness, but these tend to make the dog very sleepy.

To avoid getting dog hair all over the car, and to make cleaning up after a carsick dog easier, cover the area with a washable old blanket, towels, or the like. Any dog will occasionally get carsick. As a precaution, don't feed your dog for two hours before taking it on a long trip.

If most of a dog's car trips are to the vet, he will inevitably begin to associate the car with that unpleasant experience. Try taking the dog on trips to someplace enjoyable. Take puppies on numerous short trips to get them used to riding in the car.

Extended car trips of a day or longer pose special problems. Be sure to stop for twenty minutes or so every few hours to exercise the dog and offer it water—always carry food, water, and dishes. Feed the dog only when you have stopped for the day. Your dog will do best if his diet on the road is the same as his diet at home. At rest stops, campgrounds, and everywhere else, keep the dog on a leash. Bring along your dog's favorite blanket and a toy or two.

A surprising number of motels allow you to bring dogs, but always call in advance to get details. A very helpful publication called *Touring with Towser* lists these establishments. For a copy of this booklet, published by the manufacturer of Gaines and Ken-L Ration dog foods, send $1.50 to Professional Services, Box 877, Young America, MN 55399. If you are planning a camping trip, use a campground directory to check on the requirements for dogs. Many popular travel destinations such as Disneyworld offer special accommodations for pets—call in advance for information.

Avoid leaving your dog alone in a motel room, since this is when a dog is most likely to be destructive or noisy. If you must leave the dog in the room, put the "Do Not Disturb" sign on the door so that the housekeeping staff doesn't go in.

Air travel. Airlines vary in their requirements for dogs—call well in advance for details and make arrangements. Generally, if a dog is small enough for a carrier that can fit under a seat, it can travel with its owner in the passenger compartment. Most dogs are far too large for this, however, and must travel in carriers in the baggage compartment instead. The baggage compartment is heated and pressurized, so it's perfectly safe for your pet. The airline will require certificates of good health and rabies vaccination before accepting your dog for transport.

Recent health and rabies certificates are needed for dogs traveling to Canada from the U.S. If your dog is going abroad, call the destination embassy or consulate well in advance for information; some countries' regulations are quite strict.

The travel carrier or crate should be large enough to hold the dog comfortably with room to stand up and turn around. It should be sturdy and adequately ventilated. Most airlines can make arrangements for you to rent a crate of the correct size.

Dogs are splendid auto passengers. An added cage gives you—and your dog—security and space.

Unless your dog will fly often, this is probably the least expensive and most convenient way to obtain a crate.

Air travel is often traumatic for dogs. Discuss the matter with your vet who will probably suggest that the dog not be fed for a few hours before the flight. The vet may also prescribe a light tranquilizer.

Boarding your dog. Sometimes your dog just can't come along with you. In such cases, you may need to board the dog.

To find a reliable kennel, check your telephone directory and ask your vet and fellow dog owners for a reference. You can also contact the American Boarding Kennels Association at 4574 Galley Road, Colorado Springs, CO 80915 for the names of kennels near you. For help in picking the right kennel, order ABKA's publication "How to Select a Boarding Kennel." The cost is $3.50.

A good boarding kennel offers clean, spacious quarters in a caring atmosphere. The spaces are well-ventilated, odor-free, insect-free, sanitary, and temperature-controlled. Each dog has its own quarters with its own water and food bowls, and there is a large, secure exercise area. Be sure to tell the staff about your dog's usual diet and exercise routine. If your dog needs any medication, be sure to bring it along with written instructions about how to administer it. Of course, provide the kennel with the name of your vet and your complete travel itinerary.

Plan kennel stays as far in advance as possible. Most kennels require advance reservations, particularly at vacation and holi-

Always keep a window cracked when leaving a dog in the car—even for just a minute.

day periods. Your dog won't be admitted to the kennel without certificates of vaccination and good health from his vet. If your dog has not been vaccinated against kennel cough, have it done before a kennel stay. The cost of a kennel stay varies from place to place and with the length of the stay and the attention the dog needs.

No matter how fine the boarding kennel, your dog will miss you. He is likely to be depressed, not eat much, and have digestive upsets while in the kennel, which means he may well lose weight while you are away. Within reason, this is normal and is not an indication of poor treatment by the kennel. And just remember, your dog will feel better the instant he sees you.

CHAPTER SIX
General Medical Care

Healthy, well-loved dogs still sometimes get sick or injured. You can easily deal with many minor illnesses and injuries on your own. Always check with your veterinarian, however, if the problem seems serious or doesn't go away quickly, or if you have any doubts at all about the proper treatment.

CANINE MEDICINE CHEST
Every dog owner should keep a few basic health-care items on hand. These include:

- small, sharp scissors
- sterile gauze pads
- sterile cotton balls
- adhesive bandage tape
- elastic (Ace) bandage
- triple antibiotic cream
- hydrogen peroxide
- activated charcoal
- rubbing alcohol
- eye dropper
- plastic liquid syringe
- pink bismuth liquid (Pepto-Bismol)
- Kaopectate
- baby aspirin
- rectal thermometer
- tweezers

It's sometimes hard to tell if your dog is ill or hurt, and if so, how severely. Start by knowing your dog. Often owners notice that the dog is somehow "off" before more obvious symptoms appear. If your dog seems under the weather, keep a close eye on him. Dogs are very stoic about pain. Your dog may not whimper or cry if he is hurt or sick, so you may have to look for more subtle indications. Signs of trouble include depression, lethargy, weakness, loss of appetite, vomiting, diarrhea, frequent urination, limping, rapid heavy panting, restlessness, heavy salivation, tense abdominal muscles, and hunched back.

Temperature. Contrary to popular belief, a cold, wet nose does not necessarily indicate a healthy dog, and a hot, dry nose does not necessarily mean the dog is sick or has a fever. To tell if your dog has a fever, you must take his temperature. This is done using a regular rectal thermometer with a bit of petroleum jelly applied to the bulb. Grasp the dog's tail with one hand and raise it up. Insert the bulb and about a quarter inch of the thermometer into the dog's anus and hold it there for three minutes before removing. Normal temperature for a dog ranges from 101 degrees to 103 degrees F.

Administering medication. You may sometimes have to give your dog medicine—a formidable task as your dog will almost certainly not want to take it. To give a dog a pill, hold the pill in one hand and firmly open the dog's mouth with the other. Quickly place the pill on the tongue as far back in the mouth as possible, and then close the dog's mouth. If you are lucky, he will swallow the pill. Some dogs soon learn how to fake swallowing the pill, spitting it later.

An easier approach to pill-giving is to wrap the pill in a some soft cheese or any other favorite food. Your dog will swallow it down with relish. You could also try mixing the pill in with the dog's meal. Some dogs won't eat the food because of the suspicious smell, however, and this approach won't work with a dog that's lost its appetite.

To administer liquids, use a plastic liquid syringe like those used for infants. Suck the medication up into the syringe. Hold the dog's mouth closed with one hand. Insert the syringe between the dog's lips at the corner of the mouth and quickly squirt in all the medication. Wait for the dog to swallow before letting go of the mouth. Let go and stand back—the dog will probably shake his head and send droplets flying.

If eardrops are required, place the drops in the ear as directed, then massage the base of the ear for a few minutes to make sure the drops get all the way down the ear canal.

Always follow the written directions for any prescription medication. If you have any questions, ask the vet.

DIGESTIVE UPSETS

Dogs often have minor digestive upsets that cause vomiting or diarrhea. Like people, dogs sometimes eat things they shouldn't. Overeating and eating spicy food, sweets, milk, and scavenged garbage are all likely to lead to vomiting or diarrhea. In general, once the offending food has been eliminated, the dog recovers

47

Checking the eyes for dirt or other foreign matter.

quickly and no treatment is needed. Also like people, dogs sometimes get "stomach bugs." These illnesses usually pass within 48 hours; the home treatment tips below can help make your dog more comfortable.

As discussed in chapter four, diarrhea and vomiting can be symptoms of worms. If you suspect worms, bring your dog and a stool sample to the vet as soon as possible.

A very serious, potentially fatal problem called bloat or stomach torsion can seem at first like a stomach upset. See the discussion of bloat in chapter seven.

Home treatment for vomiting. If your dog has been vomiting, don't feed him for 24 hours—he probably doesn't want to eat anyway. Try giving him a tablespoon or so of pink bismuth liquid every four hours to coat his stomach. When the vomiting has stopped and the dog is due for a meal, offer plain boiled chicken or chopped beef mixed with plain white rice. If this stays down, return to a normal diet.

If the vomited material is black or contains blood, if your dog has been taking any medication, or if the vomiting persists for more than 24 hours, see your vet at once. If your dog has a fever, abdominal pain, tries to urinate often, or also has diarrhea, see your vet at once.

Home treatment for diarrhea. If your dog has diarrhea, don't feed him for 24 hours. Make sure he has plenty of water available. A tablespoon of pink bismuth liquid or Kaopectate every four hours may help solidify the stool and relieve cramping. Begin feeding again with small, frequent meals of plain boiled chicken or chopped beef mixed with plain white rice. Gradually return to a normal diet over the next few days.

If the diarrhea contains blood, seems black and tarry, or resembles coffee grounds, see your vet at once. If your dog has abdominal pain, is also vomiting, or has a fever, see your vet at once.

Home treatment for constipation. Most dogs are very regular and predictable about bowel movements. Missing an occasional movement is generally not cause for concern. If your dog is irregular for more than a day or two, however, he may be constipated. Symptoms include straining and passing hard, dry stools.

To treat constipation at home, try adding one teaspoon of mineral oil for every ten pounds of your dog's weight into his food (do not administer mineral oil by itself). Results are usually visible within a day or so. If your dog will eat them, raw vegetables such as carrots and broccoli stems and dried fruits such as prunes are very effective.

If your dog has a tendency toward constipation, prevention

may be the best approach. This especially true as your dog gets older and his digestive system slows down. Make sure the dog's water bowl is always full and add water to dry food. A couple of teaspoons of oat bran mixed with the dog's food every day is usually very effective. Avoid giving animal bones to a constipated dog.

DISTEMPER

Canine distemper is a serious, life-threatening viral illness. Responsible dog owners have their puppies vaccinated against distemper and arrange for regular booster shots. If you are uncertain about your dog's distemper vaccination status (if you have adopted a stray, for example), consult your vet immediately.

Symptoms of distemper include a high fever, thick, yellowish discharge from the nose and eyes, severe coughing, lethargy, loss of appetite, vomiting, and diarrhea. In some cases, the brain is affected, causing behavior changes, muscle twitching, and convulsions.

Because no drug kills the virus, treatment of distemper requires attentive nursing and frequent vet visits to deal with secondary symptoms. If you suspect distemper, take the dog to the vet at once. Distemper is highly contagious among unvaccinated dogs. Call ahead to warn the staff so that appropriate measures can be taken to avoid spreading the infection.

COUGHING

Occasional coughing is not a problem—it is usually a sign of a mildly irritated respiratory system or of an allergy. However, coughing can be symptomatic of heart problems, heartworms, or kennel cough. If your dog is coughing and is also lethargic, feverish, or losing weight, see your vet at once.

Kennel cough. Also called tracheobronchitis, kennel cough is a highly contagious, viral illness. If your otherwise healthy dog starts coughing and possibly gagging up a small amount of white, foamy material after spending time at a kennel or dog show then kennel cough is the likely problem. In most cases, the illness passes in about three weeks and no treatment is needed. In severe cases, your vet may suggest a cough medicine. Vaccination against kennel cough and a related illness, bordatella, is usually part of a dog's regular shots. If you are planning to board or show your dog, your vet may suggest a booster shot.

EAR INFECTIONS

Symptoms of ear infections include scratching, shaking the head, tilting the head to one side, discharge or pus in the ear, redness,

Checking paw for cuts, scratches or foreign debris.

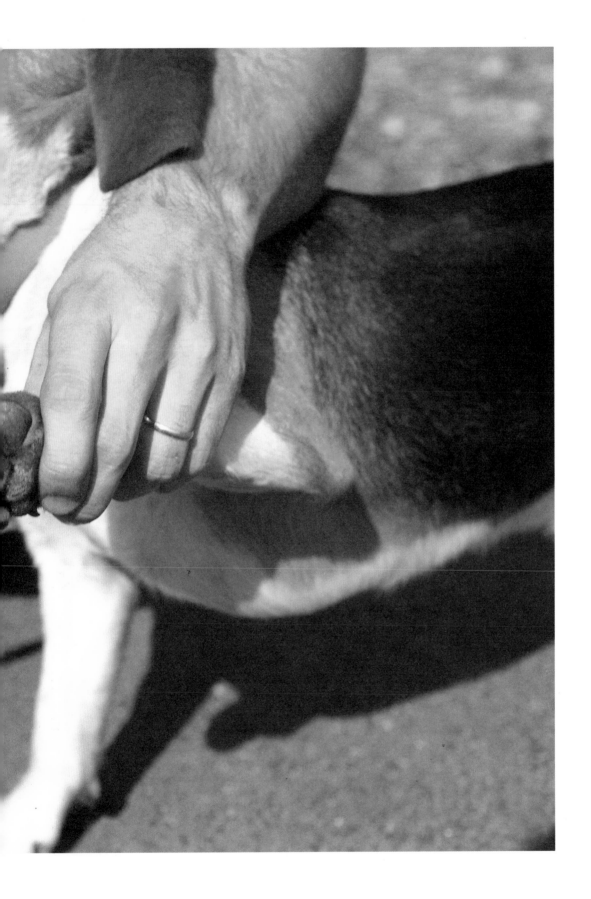

and a bad smell. Dogs with long, pendulous ears are especially prone to ear infections. Home treatment of an ear infection is not recommended—bring the dog to the veterinarian.

EYE PROBLEMS

Because a dog's eyes can easily become infected, most vets feel that even minor eye problems should be treated promptly.

Foreign objects. Dust and other foreign objects sometimes get stuck under a dog's eyelid. The eye becomes red, swollen, or weepy, and the dog may paw at it or squint. Try to flush the object out by holding the eye open with one hand and dripping clean water from an eyedropper into the eye with the other. If this doesn't work, bring the dog to the vet.

Lacerated cornea. The cornea, the clear membrane in the front of the eye, can become scratched or damaged. This is a particular problem with pop-eyed dogs such as shih tzus. The eye will be red, swollen, and weepy and may be sensitive to light; the dog may paw at it or squint. Bring the dog to the vet at once. Antibiotic ointments are usually prescribed to prevent or clear up infection.

Chemicals in the eye. Chemicals in the eye (fertilizer or household cleansers, for example) can cause burns and other damage. Flush the eye with cold water for at least ten minutes, cover it with a clean cloth or gauze pad, and then get the dog to the vet.

Lacerated eyelid. A cut eyelid usually bleeds quite a lot. Use pressure on a clean cloth or gauze pad to stop the bleeding. Stitches are often required, but bring the dog to the vet even if the bleeding stops soon.

Cherry eye. Dogs have a third eyelid, easily visible in the inner corners of the eye. Cherry eye occurs when a gland on the third eyelid swells up. Although this often looks much worse than it actually is, a visit to the vet is in order.

TOOTH PROBLEMS

Dogs sometimes get tooth abscesses, particularly in the large upper molars. Early symptoms are hard to detect, but they include drooling and difficulty eating. Later, infection may spread to a sinus cavity in the face and from there be discharged from an opening just below the eye. Antibiotics are needed to treat tooth abscesses; see your vet quickly.

FOOT PROBLEMS

Dogs sometimes limp or have trouble walking because of debris caught between their toes or in the foot pads. Check the affected paw for gravel, broken glass, bits of wood, grass seeds, ice balls in winter, and the like. Removing the debris often solves the problem.

Cut foot pad. A cut foot pad (usually caused by stepping on something sharp such as a piece of broken glass) can be frightening because it may bleed a lot. Despite the blood, most minor pad cuts (less than an inch long and/or less than a quarter-inch deep) can be easily dealt with. Remove any obvious debris such as broken glass. Place a clean gauze pad or cloth over the cut and apply pressure until the bleeding stops (often within a few minutes). Gently clean the area with water and mild soap . If the cut is deep or doesn't stop bleeding soon, bring the dog to the vet—stitches may be needed. Keep an eye on the cut as it heals for signs of infection (pus, discharge, swelling). Call the vet if the cut seems infected.

CUTS, SCRAPES AND BURNS

A minor cut or scrape—one that is shallow and not longer than about two inches—is usually no cause for alarm. Clean the injury with water and mild soap or with hydrogen peroxide. If the dog is long-haired, trim away the hair directly around the injury with scissors. After that, let the wound heal naturally, checking for signs of infection every day for a few days. Symptoms of infection include redness, swelling, and pus. If infection occurs, see your vet.

Burns. Only minor burns should be treated at home. In cases of minor, first-degree burns, the hair may be singed a bit, and the skin is red. If the hair is badly burned, if there are blisters or swelling, or if the skin is burned away, immediate emergency veterinary care is needed. Electrical burns of any sort require emergency care—invisible damage may lie under the skin.

To treat minor burns, flush the affected area immediately with cold water for at least five minutes. Dry gently with a clean towel or gauze pads. Trim away long hair from the area and let the burn heal naturally. Do not apply ointments or petroleum jelly.

Treat chemical burns by rinsing the dog with cold running water until the chemical is completely washed away. Cover the area with a clean, cold, wet cloth or gauze pads and transport the dog to the vet at once.

INSECT STINGS

Although briefly painful, a bee or wasp sting is rarely dangerous. To treat the problem, remove the insect stinger if it is still embedded in the dog. In most cases, no further treatment is needed. Some dogs are dangerously allergic to bee stings. If your dog has breathing trouble, wheezes, or collapses after a bee or wasp sting,

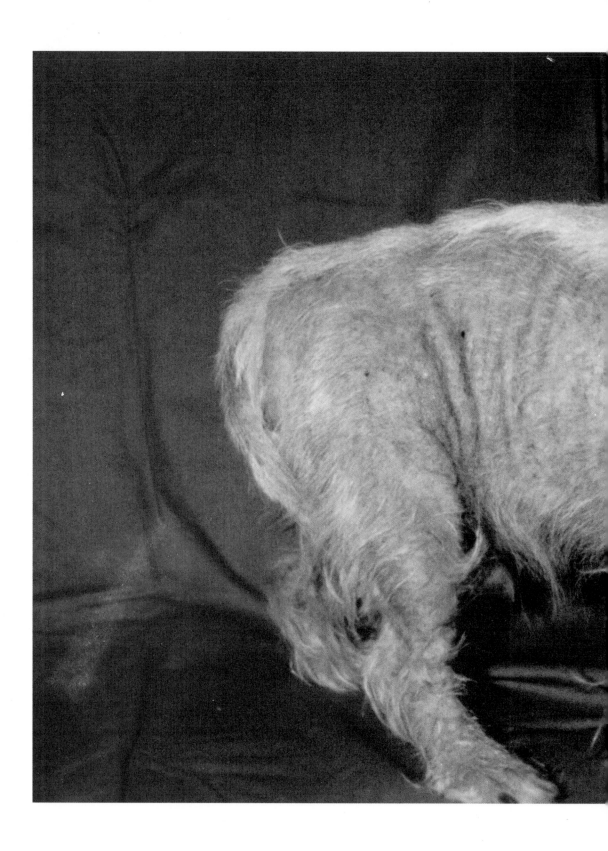

Does hay fever make you want to pull your hair out? If so, you know
how this little guy feels. He suffers from canine atopy—an allergy
similar to hay fever in which the animal has an allergic reaction to mold,
pollen, and dust. Whereas humans sneeze and have watery eyes from
this type of allergy, animals scratch and bite at their bodies.

get him to a vet at once.

LICK GRANULOMA

Sometimes a dog persistently licks a spot on his front or rear leg so much that the hair falls off and the area becomes red and sore. This condition, called lick granuloma, is more common in large dogs.

To treat lick granuloma in the early stages, try to break the cycle of licking. Spray around the area with bitter apple, a bad-tasting but harmless fluid available at pet-supply stores. If this doesn't help, try cutting out the foot part of a cotton athletic sock, cover the affected leg with the remaining tube and hold it in place with bandage tape. If home treatment doesn't help the problem quickly, see your vet. Lick granulomas can be persistent.

Lick granuloma is often a sign of a bored and lonely dog—it will probably help to spend more time with your dog and give him more exercise.

Dogs often develop gray calluses over bony areas such as the "elbow" on the front legs. These calluses, also called nodules, are normal and harmless. Sometimes, however, the nodules swell up or get infected. Home treatment is the same as for lick granulomas. See your vet if home treatment doesn't help.

SORE NOSE

Minor nose irritation is a common problem for dogs. The causes are many and include windburn, reactions to plastic feeding bowls, and minor injury. If the cause of the problem is removed (replacing plastic bowls with stainless steel, for example), the irritation usually goes away. Unexplainable irritation and severe nose bleeding should be dealt with by your veterinarian.

Discharges. A small amount of clear, thin mucus around your dog's nose is normal. A runny nose producing clear mucus, especially if accompanied by face-rubbing, sneezing, and watery eyes, may be a sign of allergies to dust or pollen. Your vet can advise on ways to treat allergy symptoms. A thick, yellowish discharge from the nose is a symptom of distemper (see above). A discharge from just one nostril may indicate a sinus infection or a foreign object stuck in the nose. A dog's nose is very sensitive and complex. Don't try to dislodge the object yourself—see your vet for treatment.

Collie nose. Some dogs, particularly collies and similar breeds, get sunburned on the hairless area around the nose. In minor cases, the skin simply gets red. In more severe cases, painful, crusty sores can develop in the area. See your vet to treat sores. Sunscreens with a high sun protection factor (SPF) can be applied to the area to prevent burning. For particularly sensitive noses, veterinarians often suggest tattooing the area black.

Arthritis

Like humans, older dogs may develop degenerative arthritis. Joints may stiffen or become inflamed; the dog may seem stiff when getting up and lying down, or it may limp on one leg. The home treatment of arthritis usually consists mostly of making the dog more comfortable. Your arthritic dog will appreciate a soft dog bed in a warm, draft-free area. Keep his weight down to normal levels to avoid extra strain on his sore joints. Your veterinarian may recommend aspirin. Serious cases may require anti-inflammatory drugs administered under veterinary supervision.

DIABETES

If your dog seems much thirstier than usual, is hungrier than usual but is losing weight, and urinates much more than usual, he may have developed diabetes. Additional symptoms include lethargy, depression, and sometimes vomiting or diarrhea. Diabetes is not an uncommon problem in dogs, and with good treatment your dog can still live a reasonably normal and happy life. If you notice diabetes symptoms, get him to the vet at once. Prompt diagnosis of diabetes is very important.

The treatment for diabetes in dogs usually involves a daily injection of insulin along with careful monitoring of the dog's diet and activities. Your vet will teach you how to inject the dog and test the urine for glucose and advise you on the proper diet and exercise program for your dog. In general, diabetic dogs don't mind getting their daily shot, and most dog owners easily learn how to give it.

URINARY TRACT PROBLEMS

A bladder infection or inflammation can cause cystitis in your dog. Although female dogs do get cystitis, it is much more common among male dogs. In addition, cystitis in male dogs can be complicated by urinary blockages. Symptoms of cystitis include frequent urination, an urgent need to urinate, blood in the urine, straining to urinate, frequent licking of the penis, and urinating in the house or other unusual places. In severe cases, there may be vomiting and fever. Bring your dog to the vet if urinary tract problems develop. If the dog is straining to urinate or can't urinate, an emergency visit to the vet is needed.

A female dog that seems otherwise healthy but takes to urinating in unusual places may be experiencing false pregnancy (see below).

FALSE PREGNANCY

The hormones of unspayed female dogs sometimes get out of balance, resulting in a false pregnancy. Symptoms vary, but the bitch may behave exactly as if pregnant and even experience "labor" pains. A bitch that has a false pregnancy is likely to have another one with her next estrus cycle. Most vets recommend letting the false pregnancy run its course and then spaying the dog.

PYOMETRA

Pyometra is a serious, life-threatening infection of the uterus. Symptoms include loss of appetite, lethargy, frequent vomiting, increased water intake, and frequent urination. The bitch may also have a swollen abdomen, fever, and a foul-smelling discharge from the vagina. Treatment of pyometra is usually a hysterectomy to remove the infected uterus, followed by antibiotic treatment. Obviously, a spayed bitch cannot get pyometra. Prompt treatment of pyometra can save your pet's life. See the vet immediately.

PREGNANCY AND WHELPING

Pregnancy is a normal process, one that usually has few problems. A dog pregnancy lasts about 63 days; after about 35 days, the dog's abdomen and breasts will begin to enlarge. Be sure your bitch gets plenty to eat and drink during pregnancy and nursing. As her delivery time draws near, she will seek out a warm, secure place to give birth. You can help by providing a box or basket with high sides (but low enough for the mother to get in and out easily) lined with old towels or blankets.

Delivery itself is usually a natural, uncomplicated process requiring little help from you. Keep the delivery area warm, draft-free, dim, and quiet. Labor usually begins with the bitch being restless, pacing about, and checking the whelping area frequently. This period generally lasts no more than 24 hours. Soon the bitch begins to have contractions and strain. The puppies usually start to arrive within a couple of hours of the onset of contractions. They are generally delivered at intervals of anywhere from a few minutes to a couple of hours. The pups may arrive enclosed in an amniotic sac. The bitch will chew open the sac and lick the puppy; she will then chew off the umbilical cord. She may also eat the placenta—a perfectly normal part of birth.

Sometimes the mother doesn't take care of a new arrival, often because she is still taking care of the pup born before it. In such cases, gently tear open the amniotic sac with your fingers. If the mother doesn't chew off the umbilical cord in a few minutes, tie a piece of thread around the cord about an inch from the pup's abdomen. Using clean, sharp scissors, cut the cord on the mother's side. Rub the pup gently with a towel and make sure it is breathing. If it not, wrap the pup in a towel, hold it upside down, and shake very gently (be sure to support the head). This clears fluid out of the mouth and lungs.

Sometimes a pup seems to get stuck in the birth canal with its head or feet partway out. Gently wrap a clean towel around the visible part. When the bitch has another contraction, pull the pup out very gently.

If you can't reach a stuck puppy, if the labor seems stalled, if the mother isn't producing milk, or if any other problems develop, call your vet. Most vets like to see a bitch and her puppies within a day or so of the birth to make sure all is well. Be sure to keep the pups snug and warm on the way to the vet.

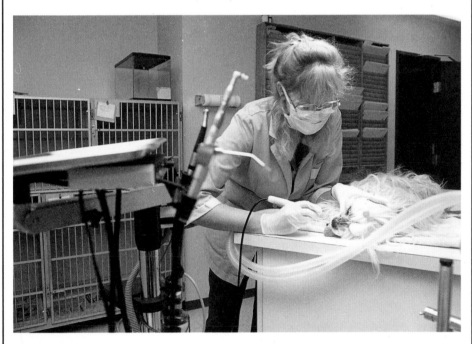

The skillful hands of a veterinary surgeon at work.

CHAPTER SEVEN
Emergency Care

A serious illness or severe injury to your dog requires immediate care and an emergency trip to the veterinarian. Prompt care can save your pet's life!

HANDLING AN INJURED DOG

Your injured pet may be very frightened and in pain. No matter how gentle he usually is, he may try to bite you. Approach an injured dog cautiously. If the dog is breathing normally and doesn't seem to be injured in the mouth or head, put a muzzle on him. Muzzles can be improvised from strips of cloth or bandage, or even from ties or rope if necessary. Pass a loop around the nose and mouth, then down under the jaw. Bring the ends behind the ears and tie them. Remove the muzzle as soon as practical.

In general, try not to move an injured dog more than necessary. If you must pick the dog up, do it carefully, supporting the abdomen and chest. If you suspect injury to a leg, let the joint dangle free. If you suspect a spinal injury or internal injuries, handle the dog very gently and try to avoid lifting it. Use a board, blanket, air mattress, or the like (improvise if you must) to move the dog. Two people will probably be needed to move a large dog.

ARTIFICIAL RESPIRATION

Immediately check an injured dog for breathing problems. Signs of breathing difficulties include labored breathing, blue gums or tongue, and a staring expression. If possible, call for help before starting artificial respiration. You may have to transport the dog to the vet or emergency clinic.

To administer artificial respiration, first place the dog on its side. Extend the head and use your fingers to clear the mouth of any obstructions, blood, and mucus. Close the mouth and hold it closed with one hand. Take a deep breath. Place your mouth over the dog's muzzle, forming an airtight seal. Exhale into the dog; you should see his chest rise. Remove your mouth and let the chest deflate. If necessary, repeat the procedure ten to 15 times a minute until the dog starts breathing on his own or until you arrive at the vet.

CARDIOPULMONARY RESUSCITATION (CPR)

If your dog's heart is not beating, you must administer CPR in combination with artificial respiration. If possible, have someone call for help. To administer CPR, first start artificial respiration as explained above. After giving your dog two breaths, begin CPR by placing the heel of one hand on the chest just behind the elbow of the front leg. Put your other hand on top and press down firmly and quickly for a count of two. Wait one second, then repeat. In between pumps, you or someone else should continue artificial respiration, trying to give 20 breaths a minute. Stop CPR when the dog's heart begins to beat again; continue artificial respiration until the dog can breathe on his own.

SHOCK

Shock is very serious condition resulting from severe injury, blood loss, breathing problems, or illness. Your dog's circulatory system stops working properly, no longer delivering oxygen and carrying away wastes. Symptoms of shock include lethargy, pale gums, weak and rapid pulse, rapid, shallow breathing, and low body temperature.

Shock is a medical emergency that requires immediate treatment. Administer artificial respiration and CPR if needed. Do not give food or water. Keep the dog as warm as possible while transporting him to the vet.

TOURNIQUETS

Try to stop the bleeding from a bad cut by applying pressure. Use a tourniquet only if pressure doesn't work. Don't use a tourniquet if you think the affected area may also have a broken bone or injured joint.

To make a tourniquet, place a loose loop of gauze bandage, cloth, or the like about an inch above the injured area. Place a stick into the loop (pencils work well) and twist until the blood stops flowing. Loosen the tourniquet every ten minutes or so; tighten it again only if the blood begins to flow again. Get the dog to the vet at once.

DROWNING

If your dog begins to drown, call for help at once. Go in to rescue the dog only if you are sure it is safe for you. Once the dog is out of the water, he may cough and vomit on his own and then be all right. If he is unconscious or having trouble breathing, hold him upside down by the hind legs to let the water in his lungs drain out. If necessary, administer artificial respiration and CPR. Once the dog recovers, keep it warm and quiet for a few hours.

The unfailingly patient dog

BROKEN BONES

If you think your dog has broken a leg, it is important to immobilize the limb with a splint to prevent further damage. To improvise a splint, wrap a towel around the leg. Roll a newspaper section or a magazine around the leg and hold it in place with bandage or strapping tape. Be sure the splint is long enough to cover the joints above and below the injury. If your dog resists splinting, just wrap the leg and keep the dog from putting weight on it.

If the injury is to the tail, make a temporary splint with a thin piece of wood.

If you suspect a broken pelvis or spinal injury, don't try to splint the bones. Use an improvised stretcher to transport the dog to the vet.

Surprisingly, a dog with a broken bone may not seem to be in any real distress. In fact, the dog may not even be limping on the affected leg. Nonetheless, if the dog shows signs of discomfort—limping, shaking the leg, licking the leg, having difficulty getting up and lying down or going up and down steps, for example—or if the leg is swollen, a broken bone is likely the cause.

Broken bones need immediate medical attention. Get the dog to the vet at once.

HEAD INJURIES

Dogs are amazingly hard-headed, but head injuries can be very dangerous. If your dog is unconscious from an injury to the head, place him on his side and make sure he is breathing. Pull the head and neck forward and pull the tongue out to keep the airway clear. Get the dog to the vet at once.

If the dog is conscious, check for signs of serious injury. Look at the eyes. If the pupils are different sizes, this may indicate internal bleeding in the brain. Other danger signals include pale gums, convulsions, slow or uneven heartbeat, labored breathing, and stiffness or paralysis of the limbs. Get to the vet at once.

TORSION (STOMACH BLOAT)

Torsion (also called stomach bloat or gastric distension) is an extremely serious condition. The dog's stomach fills up with air and fluid very quickly and becomes swollen; the stomach can become twisted. The symptoms of torsion include severe abdominal swelling and pain, along with attempts to vomit, heavy salivation, and restlessness. Without prompt treatment, the dog may then collapse and die.

Torsion is an extreme medical emergency that needs immediate veterinary care. Transport the dog to the vet at once. Be very careful to move the dog as little as possible.

Preventing torsion. Torsion occurs most often in large dogs such as St. Bernards. Many vets feel that overeating, overdrinking, and overexercising help cause torsion. They usually suggest that the dog avoid heavy exercise for about an hour before and after feeding. In addition, feed large dogs small meals two or three times a day instead of one large meal once a day.

POISON

It's surprisingly easy for a dog to find poison. The average household is full of things such as mothballs and medicines that are poisonous to dogs (and also to children). Symptoms of poisoning vary, but often include drooling, vomiting, diarrhea, convulsions, and abdominal pain. In addition, the poison may irritate the skin around the mouth.

In all cases of suspected poisoning, call your local poison control number or your vet at once. Treatment depends on the type of poison. If you're not sure what the dog ate, look for telltale clues such as chewed containers.

In an emergency, call the National Animal Poison Control Center 24 hours a day, seven days a week, at (900) 680-0000 or (800) 548-2423. There is a fee for the service.

Petroleum products, acids, alkalis. If your dog has ingested gasoline, kerosene, oil, lye, any sort of polish, household cleansers such as dishwasher detergent or oven cleaner, or paint thinner/remover, do not try to make the dog vomit. Instead, give the dog a few tablespoons of vegetable oil, olive oil, or mineral oil to absorb the poison.

Other household poisons. If your dog has ingested a common household poison that is not a petroleum product, acid, or alkali, try to induce vomiting. A good way to do this is to give the dog a tablespoon of equal amounts of hydrogen peroxide and water mixed together. If this does not induce vomiting, repeat at 15-minute intervals until it does. After the dog vomits, give him one to two teaspoons of activated charcoal mixed with water.

Common household poisons include alcohol, antifreeze, bleach, crayons, detergents, drugs, insecticides, perfume, rodent poison, suntan lotion, and weed killer. Prevention is the best approach to avoiding poisoning, for both your dog and your family. Keep poisons safely away from dogs and children.

Some house plants are poisonous. These include mistletoe, dieffenbachia, ivy, Christmas cherry, lobelia, yew, castor bean, larkspur, and lily of the valley. Any part of a dried arrangement can be dangerous if swallowed. As with household poisons, prevention is the best approach.

A variety of doggy snacks—your dog will teach you which he likes best.

RABIES

Of all possible dog illnesses, rabies strikes the most fear into humans—with good reason. Fortunately, rabies in dogs is not very common due to widespread vaccination against the disease. Puppies should have their first rabies vaccine between the ages of three and six months. Regular booster shots are needed every one to three years after that.

Symptoms of rabies in the early stages include behavior changes such as restlessness, aggression, and shyness. In later stages the dog may bite savagely or have convulsions. Finally, the dog's throat becomes paralyzed. The lower jaw hangs down and the tongue hangs out. Coma and death follow.

If your dog's vaccinations are up to date, rabies is very unlikely even if he is attacked by a rabid animal. However, should your dog encounter a rabid animal (cats, raccoons, skunks, foxes, and coyotes can also get rabies), call your vet and public health authorities for instructions.

CHAPTER EIGHT
Saying Goodbye

Facing the loss of a beloved friend after years of happy companionship is a sad but inevitable part of having a dog.

YOUR AGING DOG

As your dog ages, his body changes. Arthritis, digestive system ailments and kidney problems may develop; female dogs in particular may develop bladder problems. Because your dog is now less active, it may be time to change his diet to prevent obesity. Discuss the symptoms of age with your vet. Much can be done to relieve the symptoms of age-related problems.

HEARING AND EYESIGHT

Many older dogs become deaf. Most deaf dogs manage very nicely in familiar surroundings. A deaf dog can't hear you call, however, and can't hear possible hazards such as automobiles so avoid letting the dog wander off on his own.

As your dog ages, his eyes take on a bluish cast. This is a natural part of the aging process and does not mean he is losing his sight. In fact, most dogs retain good eyesight throughout their lives. A whitish look in one or both eyes may indicate a cataract, which can cause blindness. Some breeds, including golden retrievers, poodles and cocker spaniels are more susceptible to cataracts than others. Although surgery can help cataracts, most vets advise against it for older dogs.

PREPARING FOR THE END

According to many vets, a 15-year-old dog is about the equivalent of a 76-year-old person. Even with the best of care and all the love possible, most dogs don't live much more than 15 or 16 years; very large dogs have a shorter life expectancy.

Often an older dog remains basically comfortable until he simply passes away quietly in the night. Sometimes, however, an older dog has an incurable illness or has stopped responding well to treatment. At this point, loving owners must consult with the veterinarian and consider euthanasia to relieve pointless suffering.

Euthanasia is sometimes called "putting the dog to sleep."

If you have the space, give you dog a home of his own—he'll be thrilled.

The expression is apt, for that is exactly what happens. A veterinarian gives the dog a painless injection of anesthesia; the dog dies quietly and painlessly almost immediately. To minimize the distress to you and your dog, many veterinarians will make arrangements to perform euthanasia in your home instead of the clinic.

GRIEVING FOR YOUR DOG

The loss of a pet can be like the loss of a human family member or friend, and the grieving process can be much the same. There's no reason to feel guilty or silly about grieving for your dog. It's perfectly normal.

Many bereaved pet owners find that it helps to talk with someone who understands and supports how they feel. Your vet, local animal welfare organization, or pet cemetery can probably refer you to a nearby pet loss support group. For more help, contact the Pet Loss Foundation at 1312 French Road, Buffalo, NY 14043. The phone number is (513) 932-2270. In addition, the University of California at Davis has a pet loss support hotline. The number is (916) 752-4200.

Disposal options. You have several options for disposing of your dog's body. You can choose burial in a pet cemetery, cremation, home burial, or a disposal service. Most veterinarians provide a disposal service that is usually, but not always, cremation. Many pet owners prefer the more personal service provided by a pet cemetery. Even if you opt for home burial, the trained staff of the cemetery can provide many of the services usually provided to humans by a funeral home. To locate a pet cemetery near you, check the phone book or contact the International Association of Pet Cemeteries, 5055 Route 11, Ellenburg Depot, NY 12935. The phone number is (518) 594-3000.

REMEMBERING YOUR DOG

As your grief passes naturally over time, you will remember the many happy times you enjoyed with your dog. You may begin to think about getting another dog. Go ahead! Years of joyous companionship are in store for you and your new dog.

Organizations for Dog Lovers

The organizations listed below are useful sources for more information.

American Boarding Kennels Association, Inc.
4575 Galley Road, Suite 400A
Colorado Springs, CO 80915
(719) 591-1113

American Grooming Shop Association
4575 Galley Road, Suite 400A
Colorado Springs, CO 80915
(719) 570-7788

American Kennel Club
51 Madison Avenue
New York, NY 10010
(212) 696-8321

American Pet Products Manufacturers Association
511 Harwood Building
Scarsdale, NY 10583
(914) 472-1103

Independent Pet and Animal Transportation Association
Box 1923
Arvada, CO 80001

International Association of Pet Cemeteries
Box 1346
South Bend, IN 46624
(219) 277-1115

Children and dogs often become best of friends.

International Society of Canine Cosmetology
c/o Pam Lauritzen & Co.
2702 Covington Drive
Garland, TX 75040
(214) 414-9715

National Dog Groomers Association of America, Inc.
Box 101
Clark, PA 16113
(412) 962-2711

Pet Food Institute
1101 Connecticut Avenue NW, suite 700
Washington, DC 20036
(202) 857-1120

Pet Loss Foundation
1312 French Road, suite A23
Buffalo, NY 14043
(513) 932-2270

Humane Societies

These organizations are devoted to educating the public about the proper care of animals and caring for unwanted animals.

The American Humane Association
63 Inverness Drive East
Englewood, CO 80112
(303) 792-9900

Animal Protection Institute
Box 22505
2831 Fruit Ridge Road
Sacramento, CA 95822
(916) 731-5521

Friends of Animals, Inc.
11 West 60th Street
New York, NY 10023
(212) 247-8120

The Fund for Animals, Inc.
200 West 57th Street
New York, NY 10019
(212) 246-2096

The Humane Society of the United States
2100 L Street NW
Washington, DC 20037
(202) 452-1100

World Society for the Protection of Animals
29 Perkins Street
Boston, MA 02130
(617) 522-7000

An assortment of doggie biscuits and treats.

Periodicals for Dog Lovers

Dog
4977 Midway Lane
Marshall, WI 53559

Dog Fancy
Fancy Publications Inc.
2401 Beverly Boulevard
Los Angeles, CA 90057
(213) 385-2222

Dogs in Canada
43 Railside Road
Don Mills, Ontario M3A 3L9

Dogs USA
Fancy Publications Inc.
2401 Beverly Boulevard
Los Angeles, CA 90057
(213) 385-2222

Dog World
29 North Wacker Drive
Chicago, IL 60606
(312) 726-2802

Pure-Bred Dogs
American Kennel Club
51 Madison Avenue
New York, NY 10010

Official American Kennel Club Breeds

The American Kennel Club recognizes 130 different breeds. Some popular breeds such as border collies, shar pei, and Cavalier King Charles spaniels have not yet been given AKC breed status. The breeds are organized into seven groups based on the original function and appearance of the dogs, as follows:

Sporting group. Dogs that point, retrieve, and flush gamebirds.
Hound group. Dogs that hunt by sight or by following scent trails.
Working group. Dogs that guard, pull sleds, lead the blind, and the like.
Herding group. Dogs that herd sheep and cattle.
Terrier group. Dogs that were originally bred to hunt small game in underground burrows.
Toy group. Small dogs bred as pets and lapdogs.
Nonsporting group. Assorted companion dogs that don't fit into any of the above groups.

SPORTING GROUP
Brittany
Pointer
Pointer, German shorthaired
Pointer, German wirehaired
Retriever, Chesapeake Bay
Retriever, curly-coated
Retriever, flat-coated
Retriever, golden
Retriever, Labrador
Setter, English
Setter, Gordon
Setter, Irish
Spaniel, American water
Spaniel, Clumber
Spaniel, cocker
Spaniel, English cocker
Spaniel, English springer

A dog is happiest when intimately attached to his or her owner.

Spaniel, field
Spaniel, Irish water
Spaniel, Sussex
Spaniel, Welsh springer
Vizsla
Weimaraner
Wirehaired pointing griffon

HOUND GROUP
Afghan hound
Basenji
Basset hound
Beagle
Bloodhound
Borzoi
Coonhound, black and tan
Dachshund
Deerhound, Scottish
Foxhound, American
Foxhound, English
Greyhound
Harrier
Ibizan hound
Norwegian elkhound
Otter hound
Pharaoh hound
Rhodesian ridgeback
Saluki
Whippet

WORKING GROUP
Akita
Alaska mamalute
Bernese mountain dog
Boxer
Bullmastiff
Doberman pinscher
Great Dane
Great Pyrenees
Komondor
Kuvasz
Mastiff
Newfoundland
Portuguese water dog
Rottweiler

St. Bernard
Samoyed
Schnauzer, giant
Schnauzer, standard
Siberian husky

HERDING GROUP
Australian cattle dog
Belgian Malinois
Belgian sheepdog
Belgian Tervuren
Bouvier des Flandres
Briard
Collie
German shepherd dog
Old English sheepdog
Puli
Shetland sheepdog
Welsh corgi, Cardigan
Welsh corgi, Pembroke

TERRIER GROUP
Airedale
American Staffordshire terrier
Australian terrier
Bedlington terrier
Border terrier
Bull terrier
Cairn terrier
Dandie Dimont terrier
Fox terrier
Irish terrier
Kerry blue terrier
Lakeland terrier
Manchester terrier (standard)
Norfolk terrier
Norwich terrier
Scottish terrier
Sealyham terrier
Skye terrier
Soft-coated wheaten terrier
Staffordshire bull terrier
Welsh terrier
West Highland white terrier

All dogs, even when puppies are very social by nature.

TOY GROUP
Affenpinscher
Brussels griffon
Chihuahua
English toy spaniel
Italian greyhound
Japanese chin
Maltese
Manchester terrier (toy)
Miniature pinscher
Papillon
Pekingnese
Pomeranian
Poodle (toy)
Pug
Shih tzu
Silky terrier
Yorkshire terrier

NONSPORTING GROUP
Bichon frise
Boston terrier
Bulldog
Chow chow
Dalmatian
French bulldog
Keeshond
Lhasa apso
Poodle
Schipperke
Tibetan spaniel
Tibetan terrier

The End

(almost. . .)

PICPOUL
DE PINET

THE WHITE MEDITERRANEAN VINEYARDS OF THE LANGUEDOC

PICPOUL DE PINET

THE WHITE MEDITERRANEAN VINEYARDS OF THE LANGUEDOC

TEXTS MARC MÉDEVIELLE - PHOTOGRAPHS EMMANUEL PERRIN

HISTORY OF THE PIQUEPOUL GRAPE

THE SIGNATURE OF THE TERROIR 50

HISTORY OF THE PIQUEPOUL GRAPE

PIQUEPOUL, FROM BLACK TO GRAY

The Piquepoul grape was originally black and played a key role in southern French winegrowing, from the Rhône Valley to the Roussillon, until the early 20th century. It was then rapidly overtaken by the black grape varieties that arrived from Spain, among them the Carignan, the Grenache and the Mourvèdre. Why was that? And what led the Piquepoul to seek refuge on the borders of the Etang de Thau, so escaping the fate that awaited so many of its native counterparts? The answer lies in a tortuous quest for survival.

Piquepoule noire.

The Piquepoul grape was originally black,
as represented here by Lyon painter Eugène Grobon
in L'Ampélographie de Victor Rendu published in 1857.

View of the port of Sète in 1849 by Hamburg-born artist Julius
Hintz. The port was founded in the late 17th century and
served as a launch pad for exports of Languedoc wines
to Amsterdam and the Baltic countries.

A NATIVE
GRAPE VARIETY

Piquepoul and Pinet form a pair, so inseparable that it's tempting to believe that Piquepoul is a native of Pinet, a vine that suddenly sprung out of the local soils and has remained there ever since. This would explain why it is practically only found in Pinet, where it continues to enjoy an untroubled reign as a stand-alone varietal, surrounded by the predominantly blending grapes of the Languedoc AOC.

The truth is rather more complex. Contrary to what one might read in 19th century treaties of ampelography (encyclopedias of grape varieties) the Piquepoul in fact enjoyed a broad sphere of influence. It is first mentioned at the end of the 14th century in a land lease agreement for a square plot of vines in Toulouse. It then reappears in 1600 in *Théâtre d'agriculture et mesnage des Champs*: an overview of agriculture and land management by a French agricultural pioneer and Protestant nobleman from the Ardèche called Olivier de Serres. We find the Piquepoul cited alongside the Pinot Bourguignon as among the grapes "most widely used in various parts of this realm". Piquepoul cultivation by then extended from the southern banks of the River Rhone to the Cévennes region, the Roussillon, the upper valley of the Aude and to Albi and beyond. Cereal cropping still prevailed and olive groves remained more common than vineyards – it would be another two centuries before vine growing really took off. The Piquepoul meanwhile not only coexisted with other varietals but flourished to such a degree that in many places it came to represent the "very basis of the harvest" right up until the 1850s.

Equally if not more surprising, the Piquepoul was originally a black grape – hence the vernacular name *Picapoll nigri* that appears in the Toulouse feudal contract of 1384 (drafted entirely in the *langue d'oc*). Hence also the description of the Piquepoul by English philosopher John Locke when he exiled himself to Montpellier in 1674: "Piquepoul, black and very sweet, good for wine and for eating." Two years later, the Piquepoul is one of the dark-skinned grapes listed for the Languedoc in a treatise on the flora of Montpellier by French botanist Pierre Magnol. It is cited alongside the Aspiran, the Cinsault, the Terret and the Œillade – the four grape varieties that in the following century would make the village of Saint-Georges-d'Orques famous for its wines not only locally but also in England and even in Russia.

Today's scientists have dispelled any remaining doubts about the genealogy of the Piquepoul. A genetic analysis of the vines collected by the Montpellier national school of agronomy, conducted in the early 2000s by Jean-Michel Boursiquot and his team, showed conclusively that all of these *plants de pays* (local varieties) were actually descended from a single ancestor: the Brun Fourca, an ancient but now virtually extinct Provençal black grape.

MESSIRE OLIVIER DE SERRES,
SEIGNEUR DU PRADEL,
PATRIARCHE ʟ. L'AGRICULTURE
NÉ EN VIVARAIS, EN 1539.
MORT LE 2 JUILLET, 1619.

The Piquepoul appears in print for the first time in 1600, cited by the "father of French agriculture" Olivier de Serres alongside the Pinot, as among the grapes "most widely used in various parts of this realm."

THE IBERIAN INVASION

The Piquepoul thus started life as a black grape. This meant that in the mid-16th century it encountered competition from the newly arrived Iberian varietals: the Grenache, the Carignan and the Mourvèdre. These steadily gained ground as viticulture spread, advancing like pieces on a chessboard until the early 1700s when they reached the banks of the Rhone. Then came the French Revolution and after that their advance was unstoppable. They conquered every vineyard from the Roussillon to the Vaucluse, being much sought after by wine merchants for their potential to make red wines redder. The fashion for dark red wines was by then well established. The English indeed looked only to the Iberian Peninsula for their wines, driven to seek new sources of supply by war with France under successive French leaders from Louis XIV to Napoleon I. The Tintilla de Rota, from a little town opposite Cadiz, and the wines of the Douro Valley, forerunners of Port, had conquered the English market and dramatically changed tastes in wine.

Bordeaux wine merchants adapted to the new demands by blending their *clairets*, known to the English as "Claret" and much loved by them since Medieval times, with the black wines of Cahors and Syrah-based wines from the Hill of Hermitage. In the Midi meanwhile, nothing much changed until after the Revolution because the Piquepoul and other local varieties were simply no match for their Iberian counterparts in terms of color. By 1835, we find French chemist Eugène Julia de Fontenelle deploring the shift away from "vines that yield delicate wines, to vines that yield the most abundantly (for the distillation industry) or that impart the most color (for the wine export industry)."

Montpellier vineyard owner Louis Bouschet easily agreed with him. "Color means everything to the wine trade," he remarked and lost no time in seizing the initiative. By crossing a *teinturier* grape with a high-yielding variety, Bouschet produced a hybrid that made the family very rich indeed as viticulture became increasingly industrialized.

The Piquepoul resisted the onslaught of the black Spanish varietals by changing skin. Simply put, it turned from black to pink to save its skin. For vine specialists there is nothing very remarkable about this. The ability to change shades is a recognizable trait of old vines – a response mechanism to weather-related stress (such as periods of intense cold or severe drought) that begins with the appearance of a cluster of pink grapes on a single stem of a dark-skinned vine.

In the case of the Piquepoul, winegrowers used pieces of these stems to propagate variants, the Piquepoul Gris, which they planted in separate plots. In 1824, the prefect of the Hérault Department, Creuzé de Lesser, declared that the Piquepoul Gris was "to be planted separately for the production of vin gris and classed as a white grape even though the color of the berries has something in common with red grapes ... The resulting wine, when carefully made, is full of fire but not lacking in lightness."

CLAIRET FALLS OUT OF FAVOR

The Piquepoul Gris yielded an unassuming wine that testifies to the survival of the *clairet*: the wine that apparently remained the preferred tipple among 17th and 18th century wine lovers before it eventually fell out of favor. In 1845, French enologist Count Alexandre-Pierre Odart included the Piquepoul Gris (or Piquepoul Rose as he called it) in his *Ampélographie ou Traité des Cépages les Plus Estimés dans Tous les Vignobles* (universal ampelography or treatise on the most valuable grape varieties found in the principal vineyards). He describes "its lovely winged clusters, packed to bursting with oval-shaped berries that are grayish at first before eventually turning pink or light-red." He also had a weakness for *clairet*, insisting that while it wasn't widely available commercially, it was "highly esteemed in the places that produce it."

Thus two centuries on, we find Count Odart echoing the views of Olivier de Serres who in 1600 expressed his preference for *clairet* over black wine ("the working man's tipple"). Clairet, as he puts it rather prettily, came in two principal hues "*œil de perdrix* (partridge eye or the color of an oriental ruby), and hyacinth tending to orange, these differences being easier to discern than it is to judge which is the more exquisite."

Though black wines were on the ascendant, they were clearly not to everyone's taste. As the following extract from *History of Ancient and Modern Wines* (1824) makes clear, even their biggest fans, the English, had some reservations. The book's author, Alexander Henderson, was a Scottish physician working in London who traveled to Europe after Napoleon's defeat at Waterloo to explore the vineyards of Germany, Italy and France. He writes that Languedoc and Provence wines "with so many advantages in their favor, the wines of these territories might be expected to rival or surpass the first-rate growths of the more northern departments ... but they are commonly thick and heavy, and almost always deficient in the finer characters of flavor and aroma, which are in a great measure sacrificed, in order to ensure the complete development of the coloring matter. If the buyers and consumers could be persuaded to forego this consideration and to believe that a claret, or rose-colored wine, when well manufactured, may be better than a black or deep purple color, the qualities would be greatly improved." He adds that his favorites among the Languedoc wines are the clarets of the Rhone right bank, which he describes as "deservedly esteemed for their delicate flavor and aroma. … The best of them, such as the Tavel, Chusclan and Beaucaire wines, have a bright rose tint. The last mentioned is generally known by the name of Cante-Perdrix and under that denomination figures in Rabelais' list of wines." He says he would like to see these wines gain ground "… and from the attention which has been lately bestowed on the subject, there is reason to think that, in the course of a few years, all the wines of the south will be much ameliorated, and acquire that distinction among the growths of France to which the excellence of the soil and climate in which they are produced ought naturally to raise them."

A BASTION IN CHÂTEAUNEUF

The Piquepoul Noir, meanwhile, did not just disappear overnight. It retained a handful of fervent supporters, most notably in the Rhone Valley. In 1816, with Spanish varietals now firmly established in the Vaucluse, a Parisian merchant called André Jullien published *Topographie de tous les vignobles connus*: an exhaustive catalogue of all of the vineyards known to exist at the time. In it, he expresses his opinion that the Piquepoul and the Grenache yield the best of the Châteauneuf wines. "The wines from old local vines and new Spanish varietals, albeit hot, are fine and delicate. The best of them come from the walled vineyards known as the Clos de la Nerthe and the Clos Saint-Patrice … These are velvety, agreeable wines."

Thirty years later, Adrien de Gasparin, a French statesman and agriculturalist born in Orange, sang the praises of the Piquepoul in his *Cours d'Agriculture*: "Where grapes are grown for the production of undistinguished table wines, a delicate variety should be combined with a high-yielding, juicier variety …" He gives as examples the Gamay and the Pinot Noir in Burgundy, and in Bordeaux, the Petit Verdot, Merlot and Carmenet, "the grape that gives Bordeaux wine its particular character." He recommends the same approach on the Côte du Rhone "mixing the low-yield Piquepoul that gives excellent wines with a small quantity of Grenache, a high yield variety producing liqueur-like wines, and the Terret, a high-yield grape but with a low alcohol content."

In 1877 Châteauneuf-du-Pape's iconic estate, Chateau de la Nerthe, was acquired by a former commander of the French Corps of Engineers called Joseph Ducos. The vineyard by then had been devastated by phylloxera; but as you might expect from a man of methodical mind, Ducos did not rush into things. His ambition was certainly to rebuild the vineyard and produce great wine, but first he spent some time consulting ancient sources and literary works.

After careful consideration, he selected ten grape varieties that he divided into four groups. The Piquepoul Noir formed a pair with the Counoise in the third group, representing a third of plantings and "imparting vinosity, charm, freshness and a particular bouquet". The Grenache and Cinsault meanwhile imparted "warmth, liqueur-like juice and lushness" and accounted for no more than 20% of the area under vine.

People at the time were inclined to make fun of Ducos for his meticulous calculations. Not so 20 years later. Participants at the Avignon ampelographic congress in 1899 were so impressed by La Nerthe's "exceptionally generous wines" that Ducos was hailed as an example to the Nation, "a man who fought and won, his country's benefactor and the doer of good and great deeds." It was all thanks to Joseph Ducos that the Piquepoul featured on the famous list of 13 grape varieties included in the decree of 1936 that established the AOC of Châteauneuf-du-Pape,. The Piquepoul Noir, which was certainly present at La Nerthe from the very first bottling in 1776, is still there today but used in homeopathic doses only – like a relic of the past.

SURVIVING PHYLLOXERA

Little by little however, a new page was being turned. The Piquepoul's shift from a black wine to a gray wine and soon a white wine could almost be seen as part of a strategy for survival – a way to cover all possible angles. As observed by Burgundy physician Apollinaire Bouchardat: "The Picpouille Rose when ripe gives a very good white wine. In the Pyrénées-Orientales it is used on its own to produce a most agreeable dry wine with lively character and very good aging potential. In the Aude it is blended with the Blanquette to make Blanquette de Limoux. Mixed two parts Ribaïrens to one part Picpouille, it produces the best red wine in the Aude. In a word, adding a goodly proportion of Picpouille to the blend helps to ameliorate every bottling that comes out of the Midi."

In the mid 19th century oidium blight ruffled the feathers of the mold-sensitive Piquepoul. Just as the Languedoc was beginning to recover, the vineyards came under renewed attack from phylloxera: a microscopic louse recently arrived from North America that was the death of most French vineyards. Of all the plagues, by far the worst was phylloxera. Very few French grape varietals survived, despite the technique developed by Montpellier scientists Jules Planchon and Pierre Viala to thwart the voracious aphid: grafting French vines onto phylloxera-resistant American rootstock. The Piquepoul was one of the lucky ones. It survived the onslaught by retreating to the sand along the Mediterranean coast where the phylloxera pest could not take hold. In the 1880s the powerful Compagnie

Pictured here is the Salins de Villeroy saltworks that commenced production in 1783. About a century later, the vines of the Compagnie des Salins du Midi would occupy this whole stretch of shore separating the sea from the salt marshes: several hundred hectares of vines between Agde and Sète, two thirds planted to the the Piquepoul Gris.

des Salins du Midi established an enormous industrial vineyard that extended all the way from Aigues-Mortes (in the Gard Department) to Marseillan (in the Hérault Department). The vines occupied the whole length of the shore separating the sea from the salt marshes: 700 hectares of plantings, made up of one-third Terret and two-thirds Piquepoul Gris and Blanc. Before the phylloxera epidemic, "the finest Piquepoul grew in Pinet and Marseillan." After the crisis, the Piquepoul still accounted for "about a quarter of white plantings" in both places. There was more trouble ahead, but for the time being at least the Piquepoul had found a safe haven.

THE PIQUEPOUL AS RAW MATERIAL

Heeding the call of the sea, the Piquepoul found refuge on the borders of the Etang du Thau, in the *vignoble de la Marine* that traded through the port of Sète. But though sought after by a wine trade looking to conquer new markets for Languedoc wines outside France, the Piquepoul long languished in obscurity as the raw material for other products, transformed into eau de vie or fake Madeira wines destined for Amsterdam and the Baltic markets, then into vermouth and aperitif wines.

This late 17th century illustration is one of a series of some 100 engravings by Nicolas de Larmassin featuring tradesmen in grotesque costumes. It shows a cabaratier (innkeeper) holding a bottle of Picardan white wine from the Bassin de Thau – a nod to the wine's popularity in Paris at the time.

This picture is taken from Voyage Historique et Pittoresque Autour de l'Etang de Thau: an illustrated guidebook published in 1846 by Sète-born artist Edouard Thomas, then aged 23.

HEADED FOR THE BALTIC

It was not until the early 19th century that the Piquepoul, once omnipresent in the Languedoc, made its first tentative appearance around the Etang (or Bassin) de Thau. And not without reason: the emphasis here was firmly on white wine. The local specialty was Picardan, named after a white grape variety that was already famous in the Renaissance and retained its reputation even after it was eclipsed by the Clairette in the Valley of the Hérault at the time of the French Revolution.

By the 18th Century Picardan wines had become all the rage in Nordic countries. Before that, the Agde region had seen an upturn in its fortunes in the period 1620-1645 when the local white wines were exported to Genoa, carried by boat up the River Rhône to Geneva then overland by mule across the Massif Central. It was then that vineyards first took root in the *garrigue* (local scrubland) – only to be returned to fallow in many places following the collapse of southern wine prices in the reign of Louis XIV. It was only the opening of the first distilleries in the 1660s that saved the day.

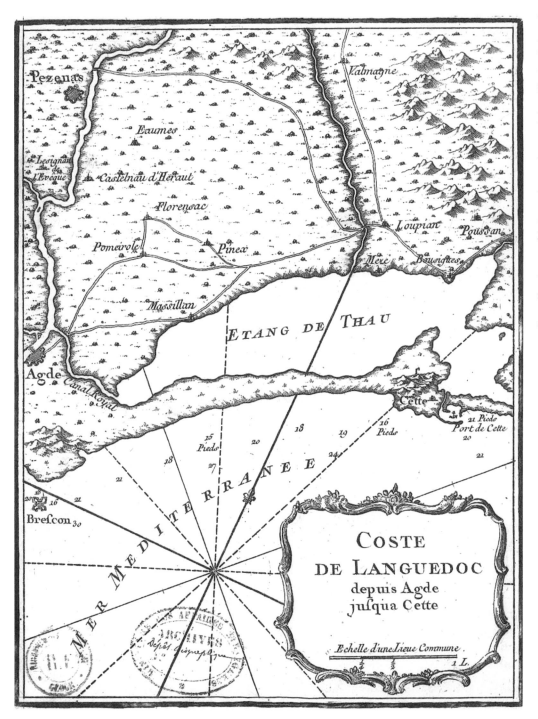

Pictured here is a map of the Languedoc coast between Agde and Sète in 1764, by French naval cartographer Jacques-Nicolas Bellin. It clearly shows the area occupied by the Vignoble de la Marine, between the Hérault River and the Etang de Thau.

The port of Agde in 1833 as featured in Voyages Pittoresques et Romantiques dans l'Ancienne France – a monumental work documenting the French cultural heritage, overseen by Baron Taylor.

Heaven then intervened, bringing a calamitous harvest to the vineyards of the Atlantic coast. "In 1693, owing to the insufficiency of Bordeaux wines, the French Navy was provisioned with wine from Montpellier, even though no-one had any idea at the time whether such wines could survive sea journeys," wrote French ecclesiastic, the Abbé Expilly, many decades later. "In fact the experience was a great success and they say the Navy never tasted better wines."

Mediterranean wines meanwhile were still barred from entering the port of Bordeaux by the local *jurats*, refused access to the Atlantic despite the opening of the aptly named Canal Royal des Deux-Mers (royal canal of the two seas). Dutch merchants, always on the lookout for new business opportunities, overcame the problem by simply sailing around the Iberian Peninsula. To begin with, they loaded their boats with eau de vie in the brand new port of Sète. Then drawing from their experience in the Pays Nantais (Loire Valley) and South West France, they introduced methods of fortification (the addition of alcohol) and sulfuring that would help the white wines of Sète and Montpellier survive the winter and the sea crossing. Thanks to their near-monopoly of maritime trade in the Baltic, the Dutch gave the wines of Montpellier (dubbed the *vignoble de la Marine* or "naval vineyard") a launch pad to success.
The Scandinavians naturally stepped in to take over from the Dutch when red wines became more fashionable in Amsterdam. White wine remained all the rage in Nordic countries and by the end of the Great Northern War in 1721 dry and sweet Picardan wines were being shipped on board Swedish and Danish vessels to Stockholm, Copenhagen, Lübeck, Stettin, Saint Petersburg …

From 1750 onward, vines renewed their assault on *garrique* and flatlands alike. Wealthy businessmen and city folk bought great estates and hired the people to run them. Once again, the Agde region led the way: in 1774 Marseillan wine output totaled nearly 40,000 hectoliters or as much as the combined production of all of the Côte du Rhône vineyards in the Gard.
Production boomed and the quality of the wines improved dramatically. "The grapes are harvested in stages, one batch at a time, wherever the wines are made with painstaking care," wrote Jean-Antoine Chaptal in 1799 in his chapter on the art of winemaking in the Abbé Rozier's *Dictionnaire Universel d'Agriculture*. He adds that while some Languedoc and Provence winegrowers "are negligent in that respect and often harvest in one go", elsewhere "particularly in communes focused on white-wine production, the grapes are harvested in several stages – as seen in many of the vineyards around Agde and Béziers."

The rewards were not long in coming. Over the course of the 18th century, the Languedoc saw its wine exports soar to become the third largest exporter of French wines after Bordeaux and Provence – the second if you include eau de vie. By the time of the French Revolution, the Languedoc accounted for a quarter of all French wine exports. Wine output had increased tenfold and prices had risen accordingly. As noted by French historian Gilbert Larguier: "In 1720 the wine was fifteen times cheaper than Bordeaux wine. By 1788 it was barely three times cheaper."

In 1780, Jean-Antoine Chaptal saw first-hand the care that went into each bottle of Agde white wine. Appointed Minister of the Interior by Bonaparte in 1801, he submitted a ministry paper on the art of making wine that put him at the forefront of wine research.

This painting by Bartholomeus van der Helst (The Headmen of the Arquebus Civic Guard House) shows how the citizens of Amsterdam were already knocking back white wine and oysters in 1655. But it would be another 60 years before the Dutch imported Picardan wine and eau de vie from the Bassin de Thau.

THE MADEIRA RECIPE

In 1815 the Piquepoul Gris was about to change course following an accident at sea. With Napoleon now defeated, the port of Sète was once again open to trade and shipping could resume. On this particular day, a boat loaded with barrels of Picardan set sail for Hamburg but got caught in a storm and sank off the Spanish coast. French politician Paul Coste-Floret would later claim (rightly or wrongly we shall never know) that the barrels were unloaded onto the beach then abandoned "at the mercy of the sun and the elements" (and no doubt the sailor who was left in charge). A year later "an envoy from the merchant house in question was most excited to discover that as a consequence of such prolonged abandonment, what the wine had lost through evaporation it had gained in quality; the nature of the wine had changed and it now bore all the characteristics of Spanish wine."

And why was this so exciting? Because it was precisely in 1815 that demand for Madeira wine outstripped supply. First shipped to Anvers in 1482, the island's wines had enjoyed niche status in northern European countries every since. Likewise for Malaga, Sherry and Port wines in the 18th Century. Languedoc merchants eagerly jumped on the bandwagon and started to produce fake wines in industrial quantities. The Sète bottlings held particular interest for French chemist Eugène Julia de Fontenelle, who described them as "so well made that even connoisseurs could be fooled." In 1836, in his (somewhat surprisingly titled) *Manuel du Vinaigrier* (vinegar-maker's handbook) he gives the following recipe for so-called "Madeira": "Take one barrel dry, white Piquepoul Gris wine and add four ounces of alcohol-infused almond hulls, two ounces esprit de goudron (tar spirit) and two liters walnut infusion."

In the mid 19th century, production picked up speed with the arrival of the railway. "Our principal white wines, the Picardan and the Piquepoul, are made from grapes harvested at 18 degrees [potential alcohol] and when stored for long periods ranging from 10 to 15 years, develop into really great wines," wrote Henri Marès in 1867. "But for faster results, we leave them in the sun and add alcohol by stages; this makes them ready to drink much more quickly."

The same method also allowed Sète merchants to sell their wines at just 3 francs a bottle, claiming that it was the "the equivalent of a Madeira costing up to 12 francs." Louis Pasteur would later devise a way to trim the production time even further, by exposing the contents of the barrel to the sun (not the barrel itself) in glass containers half filled with wine. "In just a few weeks, the wine will have aged and taken on all the qualities that are sought in those wines currently produced by the processes commonly used in Sète, that consist in exposing the wine to the sun for two or three years," explained the great scientist. Just a few weeks instead of two or three years? Sète producers needed no further encouragement.

In 1850, this man, Henri Marès, found a way to beat oidium. He was also a fervent champion of the Piquepoul grape, saying it gave "a spirited, delicate, sparkling wine, fragrant, dry and most agreeable."

THE BIG PATRIOTIC DEBATE

The "manufacturing" of fake wines marked the beginning of a decisive debate in the history of French wine. What the Languedoc regarded as its chance to escape the doldrums, others saw as nothing more than fraud. In 1826 French serviceman and agronomist Arsene Thiébaut de Berneaud, writing in his *Manuel du Vigneron* (winegrower's handbook), had this to say about so-called Malaga and Madeira from the Hérault: "These sweet wines would enjoy yet greater renown were it not for the most culpable cupidity of the wine trade, which too often passes off as sweet wines those containing added ingredients such as raisins, Aloe Socotrina, cherries, raspberries, peaches, orris and galanga root; or sometimes tar and other substances, which an art of deception pushed to its limits now employs with peculiar audacity."

French botanist Louis-Augustin Bosc meanwhile despaired for French wines on reading M. Salmon's *Art de cultiver la vigne et de faire de bon vin malgré le climat et l'intempérie des saisons* (the art of growing grapes and making good wine despite the climate and its intemperate seasons). According to M. Salmon, writes Bosc: "Midi wine can be made in Lower Burgundy and Lower Burgundy wine can be made in the Midi, making a considerable profit in either case. Unfortunately for the wine enthusiast, he happens to be right. Hence the difficulty in obtaining natural wines and in saving the reputation of our great vineyards, which is falling by the day within our great cities and even more so abroad, to the great detriment of our national wealth."

The Languedoc was not the only culprit, but it took until 1842 for the realization to hit home. That year, in Angers, a French winegrower called Pierre-Constant Guillory organized the first-ever Congrès des Vignerons de France. Taking the Germans as his model, Guillory warned of the growing threat posed by foreign vineyards "which by dint of skill have succeeded in overcoming the challenges of the climate and making wines that may advantageously replace our own. If wine consumption here at home decreases every passing year, is it not principally because so many consumers are so badly served?"

Suddenly the honor of *la mère patrie* was at stake. There could be no question of simply heeding the advice of François Malepeyre in 1850: "Leave your fake liqueurs and adulterated wines to perfidious Albion and savage Siberia; take them hence if you can draw satisfaction from such a disastrous invention; but if you remain on sacred soil, make sure you respect it. Do not deprive your compatriots of the advantage of natural production ... "

PIQUEPOUL ROSE ou GRIS.

In the 19th century, as native black grapes were being overtaken by their more richly colored and alcoholic Spanish counterparts, the Piquepoul survived mainly as a pink/gray-skinned grape (pictured here).

But the Languedoc carried on regardless. In 1874, Professor Camille Saint-Pierre of the Montpellier national school of agronomy argued that: "The imitating of Spanish and Portuguese wines is an important branch of commerce in Sète and Mèze. Russia, Denmark, England, the United States and South America import some 300,000 hectoliters per year ... The buyer is never misled as to their origin ... The real worry, rather, is the risk of fraud – artificial products churned out by factories in Hamburg and London being passed off as Sète wines!"

The resistance continued unabated despite the enactment of the Madrid Agreement of 1891 concerning the international registration of marks. The following year, French chemist Emile Viard claimed that French wines were "often purer than wines of origin made using foreign color additives illegal in France." He argued that so long as there were no misleading claims about origin, the French should be allowed to do the same as their foreign counterparts. The French law of 1892 then made it illegal to fortify wines through the addition of alcohol (French *vinage*). The only exceptions were liqueur wines, *Vins Doux Naturels* and vermouth.

VERMOUTH – THE ROUTE TO SURVIVAL

Vermouth was the saving of the Piquepoul around the Etang de Thau. The word passed into common usage after a distiller in Turin called Antonio Benedetto Carpano adapted a centuries-old German recipe for a wormwood-infused liqueur wine. Vermouth, as he called it, was soon making its way from the Piedmont to France, carried overland across the Alps. In 1813 Lyon pharmacist Joseph Noilly concocted his own brand of vermouth from some 20 different plants including chamomile and coriander. Thirty years later, his son Louis established a company in Marseilles under the direction of his son-in-law Claudius Prat, who in 1850 built the great Noilly-Prat wine storehouses (*chais*) in Marseillan, locating them as close as possible to the sources of the raw materials.

Sète merchants soon realized that vermouth offered a serious alternative to the fake wines so vehemently decried by high-minded patriots. In 1854 a certain Hippolyte Chavasse opened the first vermouth factory in Sète, kick-starting a whole new industry that was watched closely by certain observers. By 1867, vermouth production accounted for the pick of the Piquepoul crop and a sizeable percentage of shipments. The production process was described in minute detail by a

The Piquepoul was much sought after by manufacturers of fake Madeira wines and vermouth, such as Noilly-Prat in Marseillan, and found a safe haven around the Etang de Thau

Bordeaux cellar master of the time called Raymond Boireau, who divided the wines into four categories. "Italian-style quinquina vermouth, being a tonic, aperitif, vermifugal wine; dry, so-called maderized vermouth; sweet, Muscat vermouth; and ordinary vermouth." In every case, the wines were predominantly made from the Piquepoul Gris and Blanc. Though sold under the disguise of fanciful names and embellished with all manner of ingredients – chamomile, quinine, hyssop, marjoram, elder flowers, bitter orange peel, cinnamon and nutmeg – their future looked secure.

In the aftermath of phylloxera, vermouth wines encountered stiff competition from Andalusian and Algerian wines, and the volumes exported by Sète merchants were a mere trifle compared to the output of the Hérault vineyards in the period 1907-1931: 200,000 hectares of vines with an annual yield of 10 million hectoliters. But for the *vignoble de la marine*, not to mention some thousand hectares of Piquepoul plantings, vermouth wines long remained a godsend. The Piquepoul was known for producing " a robust, nervous, lively wine with a special bouquet all of its own that made it a favorite among producers of liqueur wines and vermouth." Such a favorite indeed, that it was apparently wholly dependent on those producers "with their prosperous wine houses standing proud in the city of Sète." Independence would have to wait...

THE STRUGGLE FOR INDEPENDENCE

The Piquepoul might have disappeared without a trace, no more than the obscure but vital ingredient of fake wines and vermouths. But good fortune and a loyal following decided otherwise. From the sweet wines of the Second French Empire to AOC status in 1985, helped along the way by the setting up of wine cooperatives, the staging of international exhibitions and the birth of the Cap d'Agde resort ... visionary leadership turned the Piquepoul from a nobody into a whimsical hero of independence.

Dédié à S. A. R. Monseigneur Duc d'Angoulême

View of the port of Sète in 1826 by Antoine Roux. A decade after Waterloo, tall ships like these flying English colors played an active part in transporting Languedoc wines to northern Europe.

TAPPING THE DESSERT WINE VEIN

For 19th century Languedoc producers, the temptation to earn easy money by making fake wines, blended wines and insipid table wines was hard to resist. But there were those who strove to swim against the tide, holding up Muscat de Frontignan as an example – a sweet wine made from overripe (*passerillé* or raisined) grapes. The first mention of raisined Picardan wine from the Hérault dates back to 1755 and the writings of French author Louis Lémery. In 1816, Louis-César Cazalis-Allut planted the Piquepoul Gris on his Domaine des Aresquiers estate, and made a sweet wine from the very first harvest. Forty years later, he presented his 1819 vintage to a panel of his peers at Angers, entering it alongside the other sweet offerings: Tokay, Grenache, Muscat and Pedro Ximenez. "Not unlike Vouvray," was the panel's astonished verdict. "Lovely color, remarkable bouquet and perfectly conserved." Allut was ecstatic – but he soon recovered his seriousness.

Some time later he received a visit from two wine merchants, one English the other from Burgundy. As he showed them around his wine cellar, Allut explained that for the production of Tokay sweet wine you needed musts with a potential alcohol reading of 18-20 degrees. "It's the same with our Piquepoul," he said, and that being the case it was quite unnecessary "to resort to artifice such as the addition of sulfur or alcohol to arrest fermentation (French: *mutage*) ... What you have then is no longer wine but rather a liqueur derived from the grape must."

In 1890, French agronomist Henri Marès opined that: "a good quality Piquepoul may be compared to the white wines of Sauternes." Five years later Montpellier-born politician Paul Coste-Floret did however warn of the risks of delaying harvesting until the end of October. "When a howling north wind hits right after heavy rain, some varieties of grape tend to dry out very quickly and must be picked with all haste to avoid losing the entire harvest. The Piquepoul, the Clairette and the Picardan are highly susceptible to such damage; nevertheless, when fully ripe they do impart exceptional qualities to the wines."

Coste-Floret saw late-harvest wines as a way of rebuilding the reputation of the Hérault. "It is of course possible, even here in the Midi, to produce fine wines not unlike Bordeaux and Burgundy, but only from carefully selected and carefully tended sites ... As these same sites can also yield sweet white wines, winegrowers should preferably opt for this type of production, which cannot be equaled by other vineyards less favored by the sun."

A SURGE
OF PRIDE

In 1860 an officer of the hussars called Chauvet married the daughter of Empress Eugenie's gynecologist, Dr Dubois. The wine served at the wedding banquet came from Chauvet's estate, the Domaine de la Rouquette near Marseillan, and was very likely a Piquepoul, most probably a sweet wine after the style of the award-winning wines presented in 1855 at the very first Paris Universal Exhibition. The Duke de Morny, the Emperor's half-brother, paid the wine a curious compliment at the banquet. "Even if the Department of the Hérault is as infested by royalists as it is by republicans, I find it in excellent spirits. The prefect must arrange for me to receive a few *feuillettes* (half-barrels) of this goodly wine."

His words no doubt left a bitter taste in the mouth of Hérault republicans. Nine years earlier, on the morning of 4 December 1851, two days after the coup d'état staged by Louis-Napoléon Bonaparte, 70 of their number had been killed or wounded when soldiers fired a volley directly into the assembled insurgents in Beziers.

Whatever the case, the Société Départementale d'Agriculture was delighted: "The Hérault produces Picpoul wines that are much appreciated; the finest come from Marseillan, Pinet, Adissan and the surrounding area ..." They took pride in serving an old Piquepoul wine to the President of the Republic Sadi Carnot when he visited Montpellier in 1890.

A few years earlier, the Association des Enfants de l'Hérault in Paris (for *enfant* read 'native-born') had named itself the *Picpouliers*. This is only worth mentioning because of what it says about Piquepoul wine – that it had apparently become a symbol of regional pride, on a par with the promotion of the Occitan language itself. The President of the *Picpouliers* was a Béziers native called Rodolphe Burgues who in 1879 had also helped to found the Société des Félibres de Paris (fellowship of Provencal poets) – an offshoot of the Félibrige association spearheaded some 20 years earlier by Frédéric Mistral and his fellow Provencal poets.

The *Picpouliers* seem to have been mainly interested in eating together and would meet for dinner every third Thursday of the month. Once a year they held a grand annual banquet at Chez Bonvalet, the famous *café-concert* on the Boulevard du Temple in Paris. Famous French songster Gaston Maquis joined in the fun by composing the *Chanson des Picpouliers*.

BELGIUM HOLDS A SURPRISE

It was in Belgium that Piquepoul wines first gained international recognition. After making their debut in Liège in 1905, Midi wines returned to Belgium five years later to give a carefully staged performance at the Brussels World Fair. The exhibition stand displayed scenes of harvest time in the Languedoc by French painter-decorator Alexandre Bailly (of Paris Opera fame) – the Languedoc "set against a vast, azure horizon, with pink-hued reflections crafted by Nature, and that intense light, mixed with the blue of the sky and the gold dust of the dazzling sun." And there, much to everyone's surprise as Franck Taberne wrote in his report, "what most attracted the attention of our Belgian colleagues were the dry white wines, some of them strongly reminiscent of Rhine and Mosel wines in terms of taste, color and style."

In 1913, the region's wine trade sought to drive this point home at the Ghent World Fair, spurred on by the Sète Chamber of Commerce, which focused on promoting "the natural quality of the wines". War then put a damper on the proceedings but the 1924 Brussels World Fair restored momentum. Belgian merchants followed by Parisian sommeliers were invited to visit the Languedoc and pronounced themselves astonished at the sheer range of local wines. In 1926 the first ever white-wine fair was held in Pézenas to "raise awareness of regional wine production", particularly Clairette and Piquepoul wines. Languedoc merchants, encouraged by Sète-born Jean Prats, president of the Syndicat National des Négociants, thought it "advisable" to dispel the damaging misconceptions surrounding the region's wines. "Some of our wines are now at last being judged on their own merits – for instance, Corbières, Minervois, Saint-Georges, Pézenas and Pinet." It was a start.

LUDOVIC GAUJAL LEADS THE WAY

In Pinet, an ancient hamlet owned by the Bishop of Agde, one man was about to play a decisive role. His name was Ludovic Gaujal (1874-1942) and he came from a family of Aveyron drapers who set up shop in Pézenas in the course of the 18th century. In August 1796 his forbear Toussaint Gaujal had purchased 140 hectares of land in Pinet, his mother's native village, from the monks of the Priory de Cassan. Ludovic then modernized the property in the early 20th Century. Taking his cue from the Médoc estates, he started by commissioning leading Bordeaux architect Louis-Michel Garros to design a chateau in an English neo-renaissance style. As his granddaughter Simone recalls: "The proceeds of a single harvest were enough to pay for the Chateau de Pinet in 1903, just before the great crisis of 1907."

But appearances weren't all that mattered to Ludovic Gaujal. As the proud owner of Chateau de Pinet, he spared no expense in bringing out the very best in his magnificent vineyard – a sterling performance that in 1924 saw him awarded the Prix Henry Gervais by the French Academy of Agriculture. His nitrogen fertilizers were selected on the basis of soil analysis. His choice of lime resistant rootstock was likewise "scientifically justified". His lands were worked by 19 teams of Percheron horses; and his vineyard treatments were applied only in favorable weather conditions, using the data provided by "a meteorological observatory and a wireless telegraph set."

On the winery side, the facilities reflected "the latest advances in wine technology." A drainage system, grape elevators, ductwork and gas-and-electric-powered machinery made it possible to process some hundred tonnes of grapes per day, including yeasting, aeration, continuous fermentation, racking, fining and filtering. There was everything needed to make "first-class quality products, with a well-known and well-respected brand name."

Annual output from this "high-tech" estate was a hefty 12,000 hectoliters of white and rosé wines, including a number of refined, nectar-like offerings. Ludovic Gaujal, with his usual fondness for all things Bordeaux, got to know the Marquis de Lur-Saluces in Sauternes, who invited his southern friend to Château Yquem – where they had been making wines from nobly rotted grapes since 1847. The Marquis then visited Gaujal in Pinet where his recommendation was to "make your Piquepoul like Sauternes." Ludovic wrote in his notebooks, carefully preserved by his family to this day, that he made "special, sweet *mœlleux* wines from selected parcels of late-

harvest Piquepoul and Terret-Bourret grapes, vinified them separately then sold them by the bottle, bearing the stamp of the chateau."

Gaujal's sweet wines clearly influenced the decision to award him the Prix Henry Gervais. Speaking at the ceremony, Pierre Viala, an eminent professor of viticulture in Paris, said that Monsieur Gaujal had set an example for Southern French viticulture, "which could certainly, by moving in this direction, produce sweet wines that France should not have to obtain from abroad."

UNITED
AGAINST
THE WINE
TRADE

Ludovic Gaujal was not content to be only a model winegrower. He also played a decisive role in organizing production. Though the Piquepoul and especially the more productive, albeit more neutral, Terret had reconquered the *vignoble de la Marine* during the phylloxera crisis, the returns offered by vermouth manufacturers fell miserably short of producers' expectations. So in 1906 a handful of them tried to establish a White Wine Trust. Ludovic Gaujal and the Mayor of Marseillan, poet-cum-winegrower Achille Maffre de Baugé, were convinced that "the current dip in the prices of wines from white grapes, always a good seller, is the result of speculation." Accordingly, "an organization that sought to unite all producers in a single entity would be sure to succeed and gain rapid momentum as new sales outlets were created." In the event 16 vineyard owners in the Hérault Valley balked at the idea of tying up their production for 15 years and the Trust initiative failed.

The speculation continued despite the increased demand for wine prompted by the enactment of the French law on the repression of fraud and the outbreak of World War I. No sooner had the war ended than the trade resumed its strong-arm tactics. In short, things were at a standstill. And thus they remained until Ludovic Gaujal once again took the initiative. On 9 January 1923 having finally convinced the 50 or so smallholders in his village to join forces, he signed the act creating the Pinet Wine Co-Cooperative, appointing himself as president. It was the twelfth such cooperative in the Hérault and the facilities were identical to those at Chateau de Pinet.

Some months later, Noilly-Prat bought all of the cooperative's first harvest. While vermouth continued to account for the lion's share of production, it was a decisive stage in the economic organization of white wine producers. French scientist Pierre Viala doffed his cap to Ludovic Gaujal, saluting him as the owner of a great property with a singular talent as a leader of men. Gaujal, said Viala, had produced a twofold result by championing a winegrowers' association that would "standardize production while also ensuring the consistent quality that has made the commune of Pinet a benchmark for white wine production." Piquepoul cultivation henceforth revolved around Pinet.

After several years of hesitation, the Pomerol and Marseillan cooperatives came into being in the 1930s, forcing the trade to loosen its stranglehold on producers. But frustration simmered below the surface. In 1939, the president of the Marseillan cooperative, Jean-Marcel Voisin, expressed his regret that Clairette and Piquepoul wines were no longer sold under the name of their original vineyard and producer. Over roughly the past 100 years, he said, these wines that once rivaled for glory with the greatest in France had been "reduced to nothing more than the raw material for famous wine-based aperitifs. They are being stripped of their identity, their signature qualities now forming an integral part of another brand image and known only to the manufacturer, the original producer and the select few."

Two years after the Liberation, Voisin and the president of the Pinet cooperative, Jean Thomas, would co-found the Syndicat de Défense des piquepouls: a group of local cooperatives aimed at breaking the monopoly of the "manufacturers".

ENTER THE VDQS LABEL

As French agriculture struggled to recover after the war, one man in particular stood out as a leader: Philippe Lamour, a brilliant Paris lawyer-turned-winegrower with an estate in the Costières de Nîmes, Petite Camargue area. Disgusted by Vichy rule, Lamour had departed for the Zone Libre and spent the remainder of WWII tending his grapes. After the Liberation he joined the team of civil servants headed by "Father of Europe" Jean Monnet, with special responsibility for the implementation of the Marshall Plan and the mechanization of French agriculture. Working in the Petite Camargue had given Lamour ample time to consider the plight of Languedoc vineyards – how a lack of notoriety was depriving them of AOC classification even though their wines far outperformed mass-produced offerings. What was needed was an intermediate category. The government needed no further convincing and in 1945 created the VDQS label (Vins Délimités de Qualité Supérieure).

Philippe Lamour and Montpellier economist Jules Milhau set up the Fédération Nationale des VDQS. Other vineyards meanwhile stirred themselves into action – Les Corbières, the Minervois, Faugères and the future Coteaux du Languedoc vineyards including La Clape, Saint Georges d'Orques, Saint Saturnin, and Montpeyroux. By this time the Syndicat de Défense des Picquepouls was also up and running.

In 1948, Aude Deputy Georges Guille, under pressure from Lamour and Milhau, introduced a bill on VDQS wines that provoked howls of protest from the powerful INAO (the national institute for appellations of origin). Châteauneuf-du-Pape producer, Baron Le Roy, was particularly vehement in his condemnation: "Would you undermine the immense efforts of successive generations; overthrow established principles; destroy the legal basis of the AOC system; and play straight into the hands of foreign opportunists by awarding AOC status no matter how and no matter to whom?"

In truth, the INAO had nothing against encouraging wines "made from low-yield, good French grapes planted on slopes" that were not "sufficiently famous" to qualify for admission as AOCs. What worried the INAO directors was the prospect of the government seizing this opportunity to question the legality of a hard-won AOC system that had helped the industry run smoothly for a decade. Whatever the case, the INAO remained the state custodian of quality-approved French wines, in which capacity it gave its blessing to the Guille bill, which was eventually signed into law on 18 December 1949.

Picpoul de Pinet received VDQS status five years later. The Syndicat des Picquepouls was meanwhile rechristened the Syndicat de Défense Picpoul de Pinet. The Piquepoul Blanc had to account for at least 70% of the blend, the Terret no more than 25% and the Clairette no more than 5%. Winegrower response was timid to say the least: in 1954, the first VDQS harvest yielded barely 4,000 hectoliters of wine, or just one per cent of total Pezenas white-wine production, falling to barely 1,000 hectoliters the following year.

Piquepoul acreage steadily shrank, except at Chateau de Pinet, then under the management of Jacques Gaujal. The Terret Gris soon accounted for the lion's share of the vineyards planted to white grapes in the Hérault Valley – the only white grapes in a sea of red vines. It was still the vermouth manufacturers in Sète and famous aperitif brands such as Dubonnet and Cinzano that kept production afloat. In 1953, Sète output of vermouth, wine-based aperitifs and liqueur wines totaled 24 million bottles. In short, despite the VDQS label, the battle was far from won.

ÉTIENNE FARRAS, IS THE CATALYST

On the face of it, nothing seemed to predestine Etienne Farras as the new harbinger of Picpoul de Pinet. Though he was certainly the owner of a few hectares in Pinet, his native village, he spent his time working in his bicycle shop in Florensac.

However, in a display of community spirit he became president of the Pinet Wine Cooperative in 1963 – a task that was anything but a sinecure. Faced with plummeting demand for vermouth and wine-based aperitifs, it took some nerve to argue that the future for quality white wines had never looked better – that the predicted growth of tourism would provide them with opportunities beyond anyone's wildest expectations. It was the biggest gamble of Etienne Farras' career.

Also in 1963 the French government, trusting the intuition of VDQS creator Philippe Lamour, launched a grand project to develop this stretch of the Languedoc-Roussillon coast as a tourist destination, starting with the construction of the new seaside resorts of La Grande Motte and Cap d'Agde. Driven by a crack team of high-ranking civil servants, the project aimed to draw some of the many thousands of tourists who passed this way every year on their way to Spain.

For Etienne Farras it was an opportunity not to be missed. By 1963 Piquepoul plantings around the village of Pinet had fallen to barely 50 hectares, ousted by the more productive and trouble-free Terret-Bourret. Persuading winegrowers to replant the Piquepoul for the sake of better quality wine was no easy task, but Etienne Farras remained undeterred. He modernized the winery, organized the first bottling of Picpoul de Pinet and convinced all of the restaurateurs in Sète that there was no better match for Bassin de Thau shellfish. Elected mayor of the village in 1971, he even held a ceremony celebrating the marriage of Picpoul de Pinet and Bouzigues oysters.

However folksy the approach, it marked a turning point in the history of the appellation. The construction of the Cap d'Agde a year earlier had been another watershed moment for the *vignoble de la Marine*. While two thirds of Midi white wines still went to make vermouth and aperitifs, the situation locally was in vivid contrast to the mayhem occurring elsewhere in the Languedoc wine industry.

THE DALLAS EFFECT AND AOC STATUS

"It was *Dallas* that changed everything!" So says the former long-serving president of the Pomerol cooperative, Cyr Gaudy, who claims that French consumer behavior changed from the moment the American TV series first aired in France in 1981. "Until then, no-one knew what to do with white wine, then along comes this series featuring women who all drank white wine and suddenly it was the latest fashion. That's when things really started to look up for white wine."

Another significant milestone of the 1980s was the introduction of machine harvesting. Piquepoul harvesting before mechanization was the winegrowers' worst nightmare, partly because the vine's bushy growth habit made the clusters hard to remove, and partly because the Piquepoul has a tendency to drop its berries when fully ripe. Michel Rogi, former president of the Syndicat du Cru, remembers when pickers used to place a tray under the vines to avoid losing part of the crop. This made Piquepoul harvesting notoriously slow: 600 kilos in a day compared to two tonnes of Terret grapes. Machine harvesting reversed the situation. "It turned the Piquepoul's disadvantages into advantages. With those imprecise early machines, it was a real plus that the Piquepoul berries fell off so easily."

Thanks to machine harvesting (and maybe Sue Ellen), VDQS Picpoul de Pinet wine production increased threefold in the period 1975 to 1983, soaring from 2,800 to 8,800 hectoliters. The hitherto skeptical Pomerol and Castelnau-de-Guers wine cooperatives joined forces with their pioneering Pinet counterpart. Cyr Gaudy says that when he started out in 1972 "the Piquepoul amounted to nothing. But it became popular in the early 1980s, and that's when I planted some. I didn't believe in the Chardonnay. There was so much of it around already, it wouldn't have set us apart from the crowd."

A leap of faith is how Marc Puech, the then sales manager of the Pomerol cooperative, describes what happens next. "Throughout July and August, winegrowers would take it in turns to go and preach the good word in Cap d'Agde. On Mondays they would share a stand with an oysterman and invite people to sample Etang de Thau oysters washed down with Picpoul de Pinet. Holiday-makers loved it. Our sales increased. It was all very exciting." It was thanks to these painstaking efforts that Piquepoul wine gradually emerged from the shadows of the big aperitif brands and made a name for itself as Coteaux du Languedoc Picpoul de Pinet – an appellation promoted

to AOC status in 1985 under the guidance of Jean-Claude Bousquet and Jean Clavel. Michel Rogi remembers how people tended to look down on them at the outset, "dismissed us as unworthy, sure to be bested by other white wines. But we carved out a niche for ourselves, put Picpoul de Pinet firmly on the map thanks to its unrivaled affinity with seafood. That's a huge source of pride for us."

THE SIGNATURE
OF THE TERROIR

WITH HINDSIGHT, the awarding of AOC status to Picpoul de Pinet in 1985 might seem to make a mockery of the fundamental concept of French viticulture. AOC wines are required to reflect "local, authentic and long-standing usage" (*usages locaux, loyaux et constant*), and Picpoul de Pinet had no such record. Not in 1985 at least and not for some time to come. In that respect, it was very much the exception to the rule.

THE TRUTH IS THAT 30 YEARS AGO Picpoul de Pinet had very few credentials to its name. So few indeed that Pinet winegrowers showed a lot of nerve when they aspired to Coteaux de Languedoc status as a way of propelling their wine to greatness. Their only real claim to fame was as custodians of heritage, the growers of a little-known grape with a lemony acidity that, for the time being at least, set it apart from its southern French counterparts.

FEW PEOPLE in those days would have been prepared to bet on Picpoul de Pinet. That a wine mainly known for its mouth-puckering tartness should become a roaring success was against all odds. So what's the story? To find out, we have to assemble the pieces of the puzzle at the root of its improbable success – the factors that turned this obscure white wine into the top-selling AOC Languedoc bottling in the UK, poised to compete on a global scale.

AS IF THAT WERE NOT ENOUGH, Picpoul de Pinet now has a fresh wind in its sails. With production at its peak, the ambition today is to show that the Piquepoul variety, saved from the brink of extinction, is actually a white vine of superior quality with a richer, even more complex profile than people had believed – and nowhere more so than in Pinet itself. In other words, Picpoul de Pinet is more than just a label. It is a signature, the distinct fingerprint of a terroir perfectly suited to the growing of Piquepoul vines. A terroir that looks out to sea.

A protected landscape

I t always comes as a surprise, even to someone familiar with the highway across the Languedoc. Suddenly there it is right before your eyes, particularly when coming from the south headed toward Montpellier.

The landscape spreads out before you, extending fan-like across gently undulating vineyards all the way to the Etang de Thau, the largest lagoon in the Languedoc – a huge slice of glinting water on the distant horizon, the place where the earth meets the sky, with the sea stretching out somewhere beyond. Standing out in silhouette above the horizon are two hills, Saint Clair in Sète and Saint-Loup, an extinct volcano in Agde.

A single sweeping glance is enough to know that this is a land untouched by time – an oddly protected enclave in a region too often scarred by roads, buildings and building sites. It is as if the centuries had passed it by, ignored since the Romans built the Via Domitia here exactly 2,100 years ago to link the boot of Italy to Hispania by way of the Rhône and the Pyrenees. Sections of this road are still visible in places.

The first impression, confirmed by the web of criss-crossing narrow roads, is of a land set apart by water. On the side facing the rising sun is the Etang de Thau. Bordering it to the west, the River Hérault flows toward the sunset on its way to meet the Mediterranean at Le Grau d'Agde. Such is Picpoul-de-Pinet country: a land caught between river and lagoon. Or rather lands: two distinct entities on either side of the motorway that provide rich pickings for seasoned geologists. ✺

Preceding page: The Etendoir des Fées (literally: fairy rack) is the most picturesque of the appellation's limestone buttes.

Opposite: The mas-dotted plateau, with the Etang de Thau and the Montagne de Sète in the background.

A terroir with two faces

I n terms of soils, the most recent formation is the large plateau dotted with local farmhouses (*mas*) that borders the Etang de Thau – the area most exposed to the sea winds.

The soils consist mainly of silt, clay, sand, sandstone, gravel and conglomerates that were deposited in the Pliocene Epoch (about 5.2-1.8 million years ago) by the rivers flowing from the mountains in the hinterland. The bulk of these alluvial deposits are covered by a layer of fine, yellowish Astian sand of marine origin, which can be several hundred meters thick in places and still outcrops to the west of Pinet and near Mèze, most notably around the Domaine Font-Mars. To the southeast of Pinet, geologists have also discovered lacustrine limestones very similar to those of the Muscat de Frontignan terroir on the other side of the Etang de Thau.

The scenery changes abruptly to the north of the motorway and the Via Domitia, in the triangle formed by the villages of Pinet, Castelnau-de-Guers and Montagnac. Here the vines sink their roots into red ocher soils in valleys surrounded by limestone knolls (*pioch*) covered with *garrigue* and pine forests. This is much older terrain, dating from the Late Cretaceous (about 83-65 million years ago) and the Early Tertiary (65-56 million years ago). As noted by French geologist Jean-Claude Bousquet, "South of Castelnau-de-Guers there is a sharp contrast between the red of the sandstone, silt and marls and the white of the irregular intercalations of conglomerates and limestone beds." This is the drier of the two zones, with a more intimate and often picturesque landscape. ✳

Preceding page and opposite:
Vineyards nestling between
garrigue and pine forests
in the "pioche" region.

A boost from the wine trade

The Pinet wine cooperative soon saw that having conquered the coast its best interests now lay in selling through conventional trade channels.

Though its often-frustrating relationship with the vermouth and aperitif manufacturers did not exactly inspire confidence, it was determined to get its wines onto the supermarket shelves. Accordingly, shortly after the granting of AOC status in 1985, Pinet growers signed an agreement with the Société Jeanjean, forerunner of today's Groupe AdVini and already an established distributor of Languedoc wines. Hugues Jeanjean recalls the moment when he was approached by fellow wine merchant Pierre Thieule, then the mayor of Pinet, and asked to give the village cooperative a helping hand. "He picked a strange time – it was just as we were leaving a funeral ceremony. Anyway, my brother Bernard and I decided it would be a good idea to include a white wine in our otherwise almost exclusively red Languedoc AOC range. After that, having made it onto the supermarket shelves, it was bound to become known ..."

In 1985, when white Piquepoul grapes were the only approved AOC variety, Picpoul de Pinet production reached the 13,000 hectoliters mark. Production then doubled over the course of the next decade and with the help of the trade extended its customer base far beyond the Languedoc coastline. AdVini remains a key partner for the Cave de l'Ormarine, the biggest producer of AOC Picpoul de Pinet with an annual output of 3.5 million bottles. Of these, at least half are still sold through AdVini, in France but also overseas, most notably in the UK and Quebec. The Cave de l'Ormarine takes care of the rest and now has its sights set on new markets, particularly in the USA, currently the second largest importer of Picpoul de Pinet. ✳

The agreement between
the Société Jeanjean and
the Cave de l'Ormarine marked
a turning point for Picpoul de Pinet.

The triumph of the mechanical grape harvester

n the cool September nights, the Picpoul de Pinet vineyards seem aflutter with huge fireflies.

The mechanical harvesters are already hard at work well before the first glimmer of dawn strikes the hill of Sète. Guided by their powerful headlights, they advance through the vineyards, looking like machines on stilts as they straddle the rows and relieve the vines of their millions of golden, perfectly ripe Piquepoul berries. An endless convoy of tractors and trailers meanwhile stands ready to ferry each load to the winery for fermentation.

The shift to mechanical harvesting in the 1980s put an end to the ordeal of picking Piquepoul grapes by hand – struggling to separate the clusters from the tangle of vegetation. Rapid early morning harvesting has also led to a significant improvement in the wine. Yet it was not so long ago that the carts waiting to take the grapes to the winery had to be filled one *comporte* (small wooden tub) at a time – a method of handling that in the warm southern climate was a real shock for the grapes. Combining heat and oxidation, it was the winemaker's worst nightmare.

Those days are gone and so much the better, say Pinet producers. That balance of crispness and aromatic delicacy that defines Picpoul de Pinet absolutely depends on the grapes being picked as quickly as possible in the coolest hours of the day, then immediately transported to the winery. ✻

In the 1980s, mechanical grape harvesters were a game-changer for Piquepoul grapes.

Independent wineries join the party

I n 1923 when Chateau de Pinet owner Ludovic Gaujal threw his weight behind the creation of the Pinet Wine Cooperative, he probably had no idea of the forces he was setting in motion.

Today, 24 privately-owned wine produce appellation wines.

As elsewhere in the Languedoc, the new cooperative group soon led the way and still accounts for 80% of output from the Picpoul de Pinet terroir itself. If you exclude Ludovic Gaujal's descendants, it was only after the awarding of AOC status in 1985 that independent producers began to emerge.

One of the first to join the party was Joseph Albajan, *régisseur* (estate manager) like his father before him of the Domaine de la Mirande in Castelnau-de-Guers. "In the summer of 1987 the estate's Bordelais owners told me they were looking to sell up. I bought the property the following spring." Until then Chateau de la Mirande Blanc was sold through commercial outlets. Joseph took a gamble on Picpoul de Pinet. His second bottling came last at a Montpellier wine tasting. Annoyed but undeterred, Joseph invested in a pneumatic press. Then he installed refrigeration equipment. "The following year, my wine notched up the only gold medal awarded to a Picpoul de Pinet. That's how it all started." The year 1988 was also the year that a certain Eric Narioo was busy setting himself up as wine importer in the UK, trading under the name Caves de Pyrene. He had discovered the estate's wines while on holiday in the Cap d'Agde and put in an order. Nearly 30 years later, two-thirds of Chateau de la Mirande's production is still shipped to the United Kingdom.

In fact 1988 was a key date in many ways, not least as the year when two other independent wineries, the Domaine Félines-Jourdan and the Mas Saint-Laurent, released their first official bottling of Picpoul de Pinet. The Association des Caves Particulières (association of privately-owned wineries) was formed four years later. The AOC today includes 24 privately owned wineries. ✱

The sea for its terroir

R ight from the start, Bouzigues oysters from the Etang de Thau (10% of French production) was Picpoul de Pinet's passport into the restaurants of Sète and Cap d'Agde.

Etang de Thau oysters and Picpoul de Pinet – a fantastic double act.

Nothing beat the taste of seafood washed down with a glass of lemony Picpoul de Pinet. It was such an obvious match indeed that when the very first advertisements appeared in Montpellier in the late 1980s, all they showed was a picture of an oyster and a slice of lemon, with the name Picpoul de Pinet written underneath.

In 1995, when Michel Rogi, the then president of the Syndicat de l'AOC Picpoul de Pinet, was looking for ways to reinforce its reputation, the marketing agency agreed that "linking Picpoul de Pinet with its terroir of origin, the Etang de Thau, makes it stand out in a crowded market, proving its credentials as a natural partner for fish, shellfish and seafood, particularly Bouzigues oysters."

Hence the marketing slogan, *Picpoul de Pinet. Son terroir, c'est la mer* (its terroir is the sea). The idea caught on, helped by display advertising featuring a green bottle being wooed by oysters and fish at the bottom of the *grande bleue* (Mediterranean Sea). Predictably, some could not resist poking fun – Gilbert Garrier for instance in his *Histoire sociale et culturelle du vin* writes: "Picpoul de Pinet has proudly transformed a piece of viticultural nonsense into an advertising campaign." But however controversial, the message did help put Picpoul de Pinet on the map and winegrowers never doubted that it was money well spent. Several decades on it's still going strong. ✹

An emble-matic bottle

Whatʼs the best way to make it obvious at a glance that Picpoul de Pinet hails from the Mediterranean ?

Easy. Design a bottle that says so. And in 1995 that is precisely what the Verrerie Ouvrière dʼAlbi did, commencing production of a distinctive bottle featuring a ring of little waves around the neck and a base shaped like a Doric column. They called it the "Neptune".

In the early 2000s they added an embossed Languedoc cross, followed in 2016 by the name Picpoul de Pinet – now the syndicateʼs registered trademark – molded into the glass. Henceforth 80% of AOC production comes packaged in this bottle. For the merchants it has become a must-have. It is their guarantee that the quality of the contents meets the standards of the appellation and that the price has not been reduced at the expense of brand reputation.

No question, Picpoul de Pinetʼs signature sleek green bottle has made the AOC stand out, giving it an identity that is instantly recognizable amid the jungle of supermarket offerings. ✳

The unmistakable Picpoul bottle, with its waves around the neck and embossed Languedoc cross.

On a theme of world music

I t was written in the stars that the sea-facing vineyards of the *vignoble de la Marine* bordering the Etang de Thau would one day meet the budding stars of world music.

The Festival de Thau, founded by a handful of jazz fanatics, was where it all happened. From that point onward, it was goodbye to beer (the chosen libation when the festival first kicked off in the summer of 1991) and hello to Picpoul de Pinet – as featured in 1995 on a new-look poster showing a blond in a star-print blouse deftly pulling the cork under the admiring eye of a maraca player. A deliciously sexy image that for a while at least remained the calling card for Sète's new summer spectacle.

More than 20 years later, Picpoul de Pinet still sways to the exotic sounds of world music, slipping down a treat with the ever-present Bouzigues oyster or a spicy Tielle Sétoise (a local pasty filled with octopus). ✳

The Festival de Thau, in Mèze, with its festive music and crowded tables exactly captures the spirit of Picpoul de Pinet.

Celebrate with Picpoul de Pinet:
as pictured here on these posters
announcing the first editions
of the Festival de Thau (1995-1996).

The Turn of the Millennium

I n the early 1990s, some producers felt strongly that despite the AOC status they had so cleverly acquired there was no room for complacency.

92

A lot more remained to be done to build up Picpoul de Pinet's rather oversimplified image. They also sensed that there was more to the Piquepoul grape than its trademark natural acidity and certainly enough to warrant a closer look. So they embarked on a research project that addressed every aspect of production from vine to wine – plot selection and late ripening, along with new methods of vinification and aging.

Australian winemakers, forerunners in the use of carbon dioxide to keep oxygen at bay, played their part in the development of the effervescence. As enologist Jean-Christophe Martin is the first to acknowledge: "It was largely due to their influence that we shifted to early-morning harvesting and started adding carbon dioxide to protect the fermenting must from oxidation. This gave us a crisper, lighter-colored wine with aromas tending toward pink grapefruit and perhaps more exotic fruit."

Though sometimes chaotic, it was a stimulating collective initiative. So much so that in 1998 the Syndicat de Défense du Picpoul de Pinet felt the time had come to distinguish its wine from the other, predominantly red wines in the Coteaux du Languedoc AOC. They submitted a request to the INAO for AOC denomination in their own right.

It was certainly a bit premature – at that time only a third of the AOC area was planted to the Piquepoul – but it nonetheless set the ball rolling. The INAO soon came back with a series of points that needed clarifying, starting with the wine's *typicité*: the degree to which it reflected its varietal origins. A balance had to be struck between thin, acidic cuvees from high-yielding vines and those with more alcohol than suited the grape's natural freshness. The clue to quality seemed to lie in restricting yields and harvesting grapes at 12-13° Baumé (potential alcohol), "so producing a fat impression on the palate while also allowing the grape's hallmark acidity to show through." This was in 2001. Four years later the wines were submitted for renewed tasting by INAO representatives who pronounced themselves satisfied with the results. But it was not until 2013 that the Picpoul de Pinet AOC was officially recognized – at the expense of a reduction in the demarcated area that infuriated some growers. ✳

Guy Bascou– the Piquepoul under his skin

G uy Bascou is a local boy. And as a local boy, he is of course full of contradictions. On the one hand, he has a taste for the good things in life – joyous gatherings around the table with family and loved ones.

Guy Bascou: the man whose "rare and popular wine" provided the blueprint for the Languedoc's economic growth.

On the other hand, he is a real stickler for procedure, sometimes uncompromisingly so. Now in his seventies, he was born in the Pomérol region to a modest family and has spent his professional life working his way up the ladder, driven by an energy that could almost be described as savage. He distinguished himself as a student at the École Nationale Supérieure Agronomique de Montpellier, then began his career as an enologist with the Department of the Aude before taking up the reins of the Institut Coopératif du Vin de l'Hérault (cooperative institute for Hérault wines).

As the institute's long-serving director, he had a major impact on the development of wine cooperatives in general, and those in the Hérault Department in particular – a key factor in the success of Picpoul de Pinet.

Throughout his career he acted as mentor to a number of leading players in the Languedoc wine industry, acquiring a reputation as an *éminence grise* and sharpening his skills as a leader of men and negotiator extraordinaire. Admiring of visionaries but wary of dreamers, he was convinced that the road to success lay in setting specific goals, focusing on clearly defined projects and achievable, realistic targets. In many ways he was a worthy successor to Ludovic Gaujal and Etienne Farras, two men who vigorously championed the recognition of Picpoul de Pinet.

It was on Guy Bascou's watch that the wine became an economic success story. Elected president of the Syndicat de l'AOC Picpoul de Pinet in 1998, he was for 20 years the AOC's most visible ambassador, a man of unshakable convictions with an absolute devotion to his cause. He ignored any snide comments about the modest price of the wine and always said he was proud to be at the helm of what he fondly called a "rare and popular" appellation – rare in terms of production volume but popular in terms of price. He used the slender green Picpoul de Pinet bottle as a perfect weapon for its defense – partly to bring prices into line and ensure compliance with the wine's trademark style (its acid backbone); and partly to boost the wine's identity, making it stand out on the shelf. In short, he played a large part in the development of the Picpoul de Pinet "brand" and its elevation to a stand-alone AOC in 2013 – the culmination of 15 years of negotiation and sheer hard work.

Bascou always attached great importance to landscape conservation. But for all of the fruit trees and rosebushes that he planted on the borders of his vineyards, he was no fan of organic farming. What he favored were sustainable and eco-friendly vineyard practices, a preference that in the spring of 2017, shortly before stepping down as President of the Syndicat, led him to sign a pioneering agreement with the French vine and wine institute (IVF). This puts in place a 10-year plan aimed at crossbreeding Piquepoul clones with disease-resistant vines – a forward-thinking initiative from an evidently visionary leader. ✳

An assertive style

The requirements specified by the INAO in the early 2000s were not always popular at the time, but they are now considered to have played a decisive role in defining the characteristics of Picpoul de Pinet.

As noted by enologist Jean-Christophe Martin: "Now we aim for 12.5-13.5 degrees of potential alcohol – an increase of one degree over the past 20 years. Before, the wines were crisp but a bit short, with amylic notes of boiled sweets. Not any more. These days your standard Picpoul de Pinet exhibits finesse and freshness, with mouthwatering lemony notes that titillate the taste buds."

But ripeness doesn't explain everything, says Guy Bascou. "In the past, what with mass production, high yields, warm fermentation rooms and oxidation, the Piquepoul grape could appear pretty neutral. Now we restrict yields, protect the grape juice from oxygen and limit temperatures to 15-18°C to slow down fermentation, working first on the clear juice then the heavy lees. This allows us to obtain the same results as in the great white-wine regions, where conditions are naturally cooler and fermentation was once conducted in barrels, followed by *bâtonnage* (stirring the lees back into suspension to protect the wine from oxidation and restart stuck fermentation). Technology has been the making of the Piquepoul."

Cyril Payon, director of the Cave de l'Ormarine since 1999 and president of the French Union of Enologists, takes a more nuanced view. No one knows better than he how hard wine cooperatives have worked to improve vineyard management and the quality of the grapes. The "battle against oxidation" in the winery is owed to their collective efforts. So too is "the controlling of temperatures throughout the production process;" "the work on the light lees to give body to the wine;" and the sparging of the bottle with inert gas before filling it. Taken individually none of these tactics would have produced the desired effect. It is only by combining them that the Cave de l'Ormarine has been able to improve production standards and, since 2016, tap into the niche market for unsulfured wines and make inroads into wine stores and the best restaurants in Paris. ✳

Flavor-profile: a delicate,
fresh and mouthwatering wine.

The British boom

T he United Kingdom alone accounts for fully one third of total Picpoul de Pinet sales.

In supermarkets and pubs alike, Picpoul de Pinet sales are soaring in the UK.

The wine is readily available in supermarkets, sold by the glass in London pubs and features among the 1,500 wines served to the members of the venerable Wine Society. According to research conducted by Master of Wine Ian Manson, "supermarkets have made the wine extraordinarily visible, known to large numbers of consumers even if they don't know whether it's a brand or a "terroir" wine. Picpoul de Pinet is what your budding British sommelier drinks at home – they say it has greater depth than a Chardonnay or an Antipodean Sauvignon."

It was the independent wineries that led the way at the end of the 1980s, but the really big boom wasn't until quite recently. Joël Julien took over the reins at the Beauvignac Cave de Pomerol cooperative in 2009, just when the time was ripe for a fresh start. Surprised that none of the cooperative's wines was exported to England, Joël went to London, found an importer who could access wine stores and pubs, then made overtures to Tesco, the UK's biggest retailer in terms of sales. Contrary to what he expected, "it was not so much aromatic intensity that mattered to Tesco buyers as good tension, acidity and mineral edge ..."

Following a few months of adjustment, Picpoul de Pinet took its place in the "Tesco Finest" range: an own-label brand reserved for a selection of some 20 dry white wines from around the world. It was a beginning that exceeded all hopes. Then in 2013, Tesco Picpoul de Pinet notched up first prize for best Languedoc AOC white wine at the "Sud de France Top 100 from Languedoc-Roussillon", which was held in London under the auspices of the Conseil Interprofessionnel des Vins du Languedoc (the official trade association for the wines of the Languedoc, or CIVL) and the umbrella brand Sud de France. The story made national headlines and suddenly every supplier in town was looking to import Picpoul de Pinet – a demand that remains unchanged despite Brexit. ✳

Women leave their mark

The growing influence of women is not unique to the Picpoul de Pinet AOC but it is especially visible here.

Simone Arnaud-Gaujal, Chateau de Pinet's current owner, was the first to manage the estate after its accession to AOC status. She and her pharmacist-cum-enologist daughter Anne-Virginie still run it today, now offering a range of wines that represent six different expressions of the Piquepoul grape. Meanwhile in the nearby village of Mèze, Claude Jourdan succeeded her mother at the helm of the 100-hectare Domaine Félines-Jourdan and now exports her Picpoul de Pinet wines to countries around the globe.

Henceforth it is women who set the trend. Examples include: Caroline Morin who gave up her career as a lawyer to co-manage the Domaine Morin-Langaran with her father; Julie Benau who keeps a tight rein on the neighboring Domaine de Creyssels; Marie-Laure Albajan at Chateau de la Mirande; Christelle Moret-Caron at the Domaine de la Grangette; and Cathy Do at the Domaine de Campaucels ... Everywhere you look, women in key positions are shaking up the wine world.

Anaïs Ricome is a case in point. After completing her studies in Montpellier, she returned in 2009 from her experiences in New Zealand to join her father at the Domaine La Croix-Gratiot – but only under certain conditions. Since then the size of the vineyard has been reduced by half to bring out the individual expression of the fruit – a focus on quality over quantity. Chemical herbicides are no longer used and biodynamic methods take precedence. This desire to work "in perfect harmony with her privileged setting" is also behind Anaîs' musicians-in-residence program. Performances are held in the fermenting room, transforming it into a makeshift concert hall framed by stainless tanks on either side – every little helps in the bid to bring new rhythm to the AOC. ✳

Women: increasingly numerous, increasingly determined, increasingly a force to be reckoned with.

Sustainable viticulture

The borders of the Etang de Thau: a sensitive issue for environmentalists.

O livier Azan used to suffer from headaches when he treated his orchards near Montpellier.

Then he took up winegrowing and quickly shifted to organic farming. But this was back in 1983, when organic farming was an unknown quantity. "I had to go to the Anuga FoodTec trade trade fair in Cologne to talk with German producers." Germany also very quickly provided him with his first sales outlets.

Thirty years on, Olivier juggles the demands of running an 80-hectare estate and managing an organic wine company. France is his biggest market but he also exports all over the world. While he is certainly not preachy, he does firmly believe that "a modern appellation must pay attention to consumer concerns" and reduce pesticide use to an absolute minimum.

Joël Julien reckons that they've already achieved what's necessary technologically speaking. "The game today is to give greater importance to eco-friendly vineyard management." The use of so-called "sexual confusion" pest control methods around the Etang de Thau shows that things are already moving in the right direction. Small plastic capsules, hung on training wires, release female pheromones that attract and confuse the male butterfly. The result is mating disruption, fewer eggs and fewer grape-eating caterpillars. Sexual confusion is now used in nearly half of the Picpoul de Pinet AOC area and is rapidly gaining ground.

Weed control comes next. Training in mechanical weeding is already underway, aimed at encouraging winegrowers to remove weeds not just between the rows but also between the vines themselves. Frédéric Sumien, administrator at the Cave de l'Ormarine and new president of the AOC Picpoul-de-Pinet says that all of their buyers ask them about their growing methods. "Some of them push for organic farming. More and more winegrowers are aware of the environmental issues at stake ...". ✳

Controlling weeds without chemicals
– the next big challenge?

At the forefront

A stand-alone AOC since 2013, outside the umbrella of the Coteaux du Languedoc, Picpoul de Pinet is now the iconic wine of the Etang de Thau – the so-called *vignoble de la marine* can hold its head up once again.

The appellation's two flagship wineries, basking in that reflected glory, are now increasingly influential. Beauvignac, the Cave de Pomerol cooperative, merged with its counterparts in Castelnau-de-Guers in 2003 and Mèze in 2007 and currently promotes itself as a specialist in Etang de Thau wines. The Cave de l'Ormarine meanwhile opted to broaden its wine portfolio and handles production from the trio of terroirs represented by the Pinet, Villeveyrac and Cournonterral cooperatives. Though Picpoul de Pinet now accounts for no more than about a quarter of their combined output, it unquestionably spearheads demand for the wines of the other two cooperatives. ✳

Picpoul de Pinet's popularity is rubbing off on the other wines of the region.

The sculpture path

When most people think of the Picpoul de Pinet terroir, they think of that big vineyard that nods majestically towards the Etang de Thau and the sea.

They picture a serene landscape studded with traditional farmhouses surrounded by pine trees – an image epitomized by the Chateau de Font-Mars estate whose grounds were laid out in the late 19th Century by Mèze distillery scion Félix Privat.

But things look quite different to the north of the highway across the Languedoc. The terroir here encompasses a more secluded though no less Mediterranean landscape, made up of red soils and carefully cultivated valleys that wrap around limestone knolls (buttes).

It was this "hidden face" of the terroir that inspired Jean-Louis Reffle, head of the Cave de Montagnac cooperative, to mark its trails with a series of large stone sculptures on the theme of wine. Local winegrowers seized the oppor-

tunity to show off their vineyards in such an original way and helped to select the artists who executed the work: six in all, resident in the Hérault but otherwise from different walks of life. The end result is as much a source of pride as the wine itself! Hikers may now take a delightful guided tour in the company of Montagnac winegrower Nadine Guirao, whose imaginative commentary moves expertly from a presentation of the terroir and its historic landmarks to a description of the local garrigue wildlife. ✳

The works of six artists now serve to introduce hikers to the delights of the little known Montagnac terroir.

The consecration of the Piquepoul grape

Despite or maybe because of the vicissitudes of history, nobody would now deny that the Piquepoul, albeit sensitive to rot and odium, does rank as a high-quality white grape.

It is also a late-maturing variety, characterized by winged and often overlapping clusters, and small ovoid thin-skinned berries that turn golden when ripe. Add to that a particular affinity for dry lands and you can see why it made its home in the Bassin de Thau – the driest of all the Hérault terroirs. The conditions here suit its rustic personality, the cool air and night-time mists from mid-August onward bringing the fruit to perfect ripeness with no loss of natural acidity. But for all of its flavor profile dominated by scents of linden flowers, hawthorn and citrus, the Piquepoul has yet to reveal its full subtlety and investigations continue to draw out its full potential – that "bouquet *sui generis*" to which Prosper Gervais makes passing mention in Pierre Viala and Victor Vermorel's *Ampélographie* (1901). And who knows what other qualities may yet emerge from the Piquepoul conservatory – a rich genetic legacy of more than 350 old vine clones set up in 1993.

Climate change may be increasingly obvious, but the implementation of an irrigation system in part of the AOC area should address whatever doubts exist about the Piquepoul's performance in this respect. In any case, the Piquepoul like the Carignan, the Cinsault and other traditional Languedoc varieties is sufficiently drought-resistant to face the future with confidence. Indeed it is already making converts outside France, planted by one wine-grower in Australia and shortly to be planted California. "Its story isn't over yet!" says Guy Bascou with a smile. ✳

Crisp and drought-resistant,
the Piquepoul grape
is gaining ground.

In the mid 1990s the big question on everyone's mind was whether the AOC name had to mention the name "Piquepoul".

The great Piquepoul name controversy

Or was it enough just to say Pinet? No sooner had the name Piquepoul emerged from obscurity than it threatened to return there, leaving it vulnerable to misuse by growers outside the AOC. The marketing agency argued that "without Picpoul, you lose all reference to the region. The personality embodied in the name Picpoul de Pinet comes mainly from the poetry that resides in the word Picpoul itself: funny, curious, exotic, the soul of the Languedoc. Add Pinet, and you bring together two childlike images, two complementary notions that evoke the serenity and authenticity of environmental values. It's a feel-good name, a name with a singsong quality. It speaks of terroir."

Controversy about the name has recently sprung up again. In the 1980s the wine was officially respelled "Picpoul", a name with a different spelling but that sounds the same.

Concerns persist nonetheless, and some Pinet growers feel it would be safer all round to rename the grape – as happened in Italy in 2009 when Italian Prosecco producers had the name of the grape changed to Glera, reserving the name Prosecco for the designation of origin. The situation there was not quite the same, Prosecco also being the name of a small town in the Province of Trieste. Only time will tell whether in this case tradition and the link between the grape and the wine will be enough to defend the identity of the brand. ☀

Toward age-worthy wines

In the 1990s a number of estates (Bridau, Mas Saint-Laurent, Saint-Martin-de-la-Garrigue and Chateau de Pinet-Gaujal de Saint-Bon) sought to stand out from the competition with fatter, more complex wines that played on riper grapes and maturation on fine lees.

The ambition now is to make more complex wines, from riper grapes.

"They were rejected by the tasting panel on the grounds that they were 'atypical'," remembers Anne-Virginie Arnaud-Gaujal.

Thinking has evolved since then. The Piquepoul these days is seen as a grape with ambitions, cast in a new light thanks to plot selection and a controlled fermentation process that makes the most of those too-long ignored "flavor precursors". In the words of Claude Jourdan: "Maturation on fine lees helps to cushion those solid tannins you get with late-harvested grapes. The press wine is vinified separately before blending, adding fat and perfumes of exotic fruit such as mango mixed with citrus. It adds color too, making for a deeper, less translucent shade of gold. Some have accused our wines of being oxidized, but things are changing, moving forward, customers are increasingly curious, more open to new experiences."

Thanks to this new profile Picpoul de Pinet is now finally going places. It has gained entry to Parisian wine stores and restaurants and is making steady inroads in overseas markets. The people most committed to its success all agree that enriching the raw material produces a more nuanced nose, a more sappy and elegant palate, and a wine generally built for long aging. As enologist Jean-Claude Martin puts it: "We're moving toward cellar-worthy wines. Everybody knows that Chablis, though not particularly expressive in youth, takes on a wonderfully complex patina with age. Thanks to its acid backbone, we expect the same to be true of Picpoul on condition that the wine is kept in a climate-controlled environment." For Roland Tarroux of the Mas St Laurent, as Picpoul ages it develops "aromas of beeswax, quince and fresh mown hay." The time has plainly come for Picpoul de Pinet to show its true worth. ✻

Claude Jourdan, owner of the Domaine Félines-Jourdan, is the impassioned winemaker behind richer, more complex Picpoul de Pinet wines that are winning her new markets, including in Russia.

An evolution is underway and Picpoul de Pinet is increasingly recognized as a wine to watch. Pierre Citerne, in a recent article for La Revue du Vin de France, wrote that unlike a good many Languedoc whites, "Picpoul de Pinet wines are never heavy or flat."

Emerging from its shell

Blooming prospects:
new markets for Picpoul-de-Pinet
open up myriad possibilities
for new food and wine pairings.

The keynote here is litheness. The best of them have a character all of their own, showing lightly smoky, iodized notes and generous fruit, sometimes with overlaying hints of musk and honey that counterbalance the wine's signature lemony acidity … An extra year's aging after bottling helps the wine to open up and show its true colors. Some can even withstand several years' aging."

Andrew Jefford, writing in *Decanter*, is no less enthusiastic: "Once its neat little niche offers more depth and aromatic nuance, Picpoul de Pinet could become not just a Languedoc classic, but a French one."

Certain observers caution that "the price of Chablis represents something of a glass ceiling in the United Kingdom;" or as one winegrower puts it: "Let's keep our feet firmly on the ground." The most motivated growers are nonetheless firmly decided to obtain a just reward for their efforts. For Andrew Jefford, the next stage may well play out in the USA, the AOC's second biggest export market.

And in France? Several wineries now offer smoother, more complex cuvees that find favor with wine stores once insensitive to the charms of Picpoul de Pinet. "It's an enormous market but we need to work on our communications," warns Anaïs Ricome. Picpoul de Pinet has to show that it doesn't just go with oysters, but with a whole host of other delicacies too, including sushi and fish carpaccio. In Boston it's proved a hit with lobster.

Picpoul de Pinet is ready to emerge from its shell. The adventure has only just begun. ✹

BIBLIOGRAPHY

CAVOLEAU, Jean Alexandre. *Œnologie française, ou Statistique de tous les vignobles et de toutes les boissons vineuses et spiritueuses de la France, suivie de considérations générales sur la culture de la vigne.* Paris: Mme Huzard, 1827.

CHAPTAL, Jean Antoine. *Traité théorique et pratique sur la culture de la vigne, avec l'art de faire le vin, les eaux-de-vie, esprit de vin, vinaigres...* Paris: Delalain, 1801.

CLAVEL, Jean and BAILLAUD, Robert. *Histoire et avenir des vins en Languedoc.* Toulouse: Privat, 1985.

COSTE-FLORET, Paul. *Les Travaux du vignoble. Plantations, cultures, engrais, défense contre les insectes et les maladies de la vigne.* Montpellier: Coulet et fils (Bibliothèque du Progrès agricole et viticole), 1898.

EXPILLY, Abbé Jean Joseph. *Dictionnaire géographique historique et politique des Gaules et de la France.* Vol IV. Paris: Desaint et Saillant, 1766.

GARRIER, Gilbert. *Histoire sociale et culturelle du vin.* Paris: Larousse (In Extenso), 1998. Rééd. 2008.

GASPARIN, Adrien. Comte de. *Cours d'agriculture.* Vol IV. Paris: Maison Rustique, 1843-1848.

GAVIGNAUD-FONTAINE, Geneviève and LARGUIER, Gilbert. *Le Vin en Languedoc et en Roussillon. De la tradition aux mondialisations. XVIe-XXIe siècle.* Canet: Trabucaire, 2007.

GUYOT, Jules. *Étude des vignobles de France pour servir à l'enseignement mutuel de la viticulture et de la vinification françaises.* Vol I: *Régions du Sud-Est et du Sud-Ouest.* Paris: Imprimerie impériale, 1868. Facsimiles: Marseille, J. Laffitte, 1982; Orthez, Louis Rabier, 2015.

HENDERSON, Alexander. *The History of Ancient and Modern Wines.* London: Baldwin, Cradock and Joy, 1824.

HUMBERT, Florian. *L'INAO, de ses origines à la fin des années 1960. Genèse et évolutions du système des vins d'AOC.* PhD thesis in history, University of Burgundy, 2011.

JULIA DE FONTENELLE, Eugène. *Manuel théorique et pratique du vinaigrier et du moutardier.* 2nd ed. Paris: Roret, 1836.

JULLIEN, André. *Topographie de tous les vignobles connus.* Paris: 1816.

LACHIVER, Marcel. *Vins, vignes et vignerons. Histoire du vignoble français.* Paris: Fayard, (Nouvelles études historiques) 1988. Rééd. 1997.

LEBEAUD, Nicolas and JULIA DE FONTENELLE, Eugène. *Manuel complet théorique et pratique du distillateur et du liquoriste, ou Traité de la distillation.* 4th ed. Paris: Roret, 1835.

LE BRAS, Stéphane. *Négoce et négociants en vins dans l'Hérault: pratiques, influences, trajectoires (1900-1970)*. PhD thesis in contemporary history, University of Montpellier 3, 2013.

LE ROY LADURIE, Emmanuel. *Les Paysans de Languedoc*. PhD thesis in literature, 1966. Paris: Flammarion, (Champs Histoire) [1969] 1993.

MARÈS, Henri. *Description des cépages principaux de la région méditerranéenne de la France*. Montpellier: C. Coulet, 1890. Facsimile: La Celle, Association Étienne et Louise Marès, 2014.

ODART, Alexandre, Pierre, Count, *Ampélographie, ou Traité des cépages les plus estimés dans les vignobles de quelque renom*. Paris: Bixio, 1845.

PORTES, Jean-Claude. *Châteauneuf-du-Pape. Première AOC de France*. Châteauneuf-du-Pape, Organisme de Défense et de Gestion de l'AOC Châteauneuf-du-Pape, 2016.

POURCHASSE, Pierrick. *Le Commerce du Nord. Les échanges commerciaux entre la France et l'Europe septen-trionale au XVIIIᵉ siècle*. Rennes: Presses universitaires de Rennes, (Histoire) 2006.

RENDU, Victor. *Ampélographie française comprenant la statistique, la description des meilleurs cépages, l'ana-lyse chimique du sol et les procédés de culture et de vinification des principaux vignobles de la France*. 2ⁿᵈ ed. Paris: Masson, 1857.

RÉZEAU, Pierre. *Dictionnaire des noms de cépages de France. Histoire et étymologie*. Paris: CNRS Éditions, 2008.

ROBINSON, Jancis (Ed). *The Oxford Companion to Wine*. Oxford: Oxford University Press, (Oxford Companions) 1994 (Translated from: *Encylopédie du Vin*. Paris: Hachette, 1997). 4ᵗʰ ed. 2015. Visit www.jancisrobinson.com/ocw.

ROZIER, Abbé François (Ed). *Cours complet d'agriculture théorique, pratique, économique, et de médecine rurale et vétérinaire*. Volume X (by Chaptal, Dussieux, Parmentier et al.). Paris: Moutardier, 1800.

SERRES, Olivier de. *Théâtre d'agriculture et de mesnage des champs*. Paris: Jamet Métayer, 1600.

THIÉBAUT DE BERNEAUD, Arsenne and MALEPEYRE, François. *Nouveau Manuel complet du vigneron, ou l'Art de cultiver la vigne, de faire les vins, eaux-de-vie et vinaigres...* 5ᵗʰ ed, revised and expanded by François Malepeyre. Paris: Roret, 1850.

VIALA, Pierre and VERMOREL, Victor (Ed). *Ampélographie. Traité général de viticulture*. Vol. II. Paris: Masson et Cie, 1901. Facsimile: Marseille, J. Laffitte, 1991.

WEGENER SLEESWIJK, Anne. *Les Vins français aux Provinces-Unies au XVIIIe siècle – Franse wijn in de Republiek in de 18ᵉ eeuw*. PhD thesis in modern history, University of Amsterdam and EHESS, Paris, 2006.

LIST OF PRODUCERS

DOMAINE DE BELLE MARE
34140 Mèze
04 67 43 17 68
contact@belle-mare.com

DOMAINE DE BRIDAU
34530 Montagnac
06 74 00 05 33
montblanc34@live.fr

DOMAINE DE LA BRIFFAUDE
34530 Montagnac
04 67 24 11 77
labriffaude@yahoo.fr

DOMAINE DE CAMPAUCELS
34530 Montagnac
04 67 24 19 16
domainecampaucels@orange.fr

DOMAINE DE CASTELNAU
34120 Castelnau-de-Guers
04 67 98 16 19
castelnau1@wanadoo.fr

DOMAINE COUSTELLIER
34510 Florensac
04 67 77 01 42
domainecoustellier@wanadoo.fr

DOMAINE DE CREYSSELS
34140 Mèze
04 67 43 80 82
contact@creyssels.fr

DOMAINE LA CROIX GRATIOT
34530 Montagnac
04 67 25 27 88
croixgratiot@gmail.com

DOMAINE FÉLINES JOURDAN
34140 Mèze
04 67 43 69 29
claude@felines-jourdan.com

CAVE LES VIGNERONS DE
FLORENSAC- 34510 Florensac
04 67 77 00 20
contact@vignerons-florensac.fr

DOMAINE FONT-MARS
34140 Mèze
04 67 43 81 19
infos@font-mars.com

DOMAINE GAUJAL
34850 Pinet
04 67 77 02 12
lg@gaujal.fr

DOMAINE LA GRANGETTE
34120 Castelnau-de-Guers
04 67 98 13 56
info@domainelagrangette.com

DOMAINE DES LAURIERS
34120 Castelnau-de-Guers
04 67 98 18 20
contact@domaine-des-lauriers.com

DOMAINE DE LA MIRANDE
34120 Castelnau-de-Guers
04 67 98 21 52
vinmirande@hotmail.com

CAVE LES VIGNOBLES MONTAGNAC
34530 Montagnac
04 67 24 03 74
info@lesvignoblesmontagnac.com

DOMAINE MORIN-LANGARAN
34140 Mèze
04 67 43 71 76
domainemorin-langaran@wanadoo.fr

DOMAINE DE L'OCTROI
34300 AGDE
04 67 94 77 31
gerarddelort986@orange.fr

CAVE DE L'ORMARINE
34850 Pinet
04 67 77 03 10
contact@caveormarine.com

DOMAINE DE PETIT ROUBIE
34850 Pinet
04 67 77 09 28
petitroubie@gmail.com

CHÂTEAU DE PINET- GAUJAL DE
SAINT BON - 34850 Pinet
04 67 77 00 39
chateaudepinet@orange.fr

CAVE DE POMEROLS
34810 Pomerols
04 67 77 01 59
info@cave-pomerols.com

DOMAINE REINE JULIETTE
34120 Castelnau-de-Guers
06 35 25 67 78
marionallies0765@orange.fr

MAS SAINT-LAURENT
34140 Mèze
04 67 43 92 30
massaintlaurent@wanadoo.fr

CHÂTEAU SAINT MARTIN DE LA
GARRIGUE - 34530 Montagnac
04 67 24 00 40
contact@stmartingarrigue.com

DOMAINE SAVARY DE BEAUREGARD
34530 Montagnac
04 67 24 00 12
contact@savarydebeauregard.com

DOMAINE SOPENA
34510 Florensac
04 67 77 05 13
domainesopena@wanadoo.fr

ACKNOWLEDGEMENTS

THANK YOU...

To the generations of winegrowers who nurtured then developed the Piquepoul grape
and created a sanctuary zone for its production on the north banks of the Etang de Thau,

To Étienne Farras and the Pinet cooperative who had the vision to identify and develop
a modern incarnation of this traditional grape via the VDQS structure,

To the men of the 1980s who brought together the great terroirs of the Coteaux du Languedoc
appellation,

To all those winegrowers who in 1995 agreed to work for the recognition of Picpoul de Pinet
as an AOC,

To the INAO for its intelligent guidance,

To the CIVL for its enlightened assistance,

To elected representatives for the help they have given, at local, departmental and regional level,
and within the Agglo Thau Méditerranée community of communes,

To all of the technical and economic personnel within our businesses for their know-how
and their interest,

To Marc Médevielle and Emmanuel Perrin for rising to this challenge!

Guy Bascou

THE AUTHORS WOULD LIKE TO THANK

Guy Bascou,

And each person who contributed to the publication of this book:
Joseph Albajan, Guillaume and Marion Allies, Simone and Anne-Virginie Arnaud-Gaujal,
Olivier Azan, Marie-Claude Bascou, Julie Benau, Jean-Michel Boursiquot,
Jean-Claude Bousquet, Florence Brutton, Jean Clavel, Jean-Baptiste de Clock, Émile Dominguez,
Marc Dubernet, Freddy and Grégory Farras, Marie-Hélène Favant, Cyr Gaudy, Claude Gaujal,
Jean-Philippe Granier, Nadine Guirao, David Huguenin, Hugues Jeanjean, Claude Jourdan,
Joël Julien and the staff of Beauvignac, Gilbert Larguier, Stéphane Le Bras, Virginie Mahieux,
Ian Manson, Jean-Christophe Martin, Albert and Caroline Morin, Alexandre and Bertrand
de Mortillet, Bruno Pagnard, Jean-Claude Portes, Cyril Payon and the staff of l'Ormarine,
Rémy Pech, Aude Perrier, Marc Puech Jean-Louis Reffle, Michel Rémondat, Anaïs Ricôme,
Michel Roggi, Valérie Roux, Philippe Sansot, Corinne Schmidt, Frédéric Sumien,
Florent Tarbouriech, Roland Tarroux, Stéphane Tarroux, Monique Teyssier,
Philippe Vallier, Cécile Varéon, Benoît Vidal, Jérôme Villaret, Christian Vœux.

Graphic design and art work: Aude Perrier
Translation from French: Florence Brutton

Image credits
All the photographs are by Emmanuel Perrin, with the exception of:
Pages 8-9: © Sète, Musée Paul Valéry; page 11: all rights reserved; page 23: © Institut Olivier de Serres;
page 17: © Musée d'art et d'histoire d'orange/photograph Philippe Gromelle; pages 19, 22 and 35: ©Médiathèque
Centrale Émile Zola Montpellier Méditerranée Métropole; page 21: © BnF, Dist. RMN-Grand Palais/image BnF;
page 23: © BnF; pages 24-25: © Fondation Taylor/F. Arnaud; page 27: © RMN-Grand Palais (Château de Versailles)/all
rights reserved; pages 28-29: © Amsterdam Museum; page 31: all rights reserved; page 33: © Archives départemen-
tales de l'Hérault; page 41: BnF; page 43: all rights reserved; page 49: all right reserved.

Photoengraving: IGS-CP (16)
Printed by Graphycems

Copyright ©2018, Éditions de La Martinière, an imprint of EDLM for the original and English translation
ISBN: 978-1-4197-3329-1

Printed and bound in Spain
10 9 8 7 6 5 4 3 2 1

Abrams books are available at special discounts when purchased in quantity for premiums and promotions as well
as fundraising or educational use. Special editions can also be created to specification. For details, contact
specialsales@abramsbooks.com or the address below.

The abuse of acohol is dangerous to health, consume in moderation.

ABRAMS
The Art of Books

195 Broadway
New York, NY 10007
abramsbooks.com